NOT FOR EVERYONE

Should you read *Serve Strong?*

Not if you think that God only uses people who have it all together.

Not if you're unwilling to admit that ministry is messy, and often hard.

Not if you're unfamiliar with pain, failure, or doubts.

Not if you believe you've outgrown your vulnerability to temptation and left serious struggles with sin behind.

It isn't for you if your eyes stay dry.

It isn't for you if you believe that a framed diploma from a Bible college or seminary is the primary credential for ministry.

It isn't for you if you believe that the only persons who need to hear the gospel preached are unbelievers.

———

Serve Strong is for Bible study leaders, missionaries, pastoral staff, and others active in ministry. So, is it a book for *you?*

It *is* for you if you don't always feel God's presence.

It is for you if you don't always feel up to the tasks God assigned you.

It is if you know what it's like to come to the end of yourself.

You'll want to read it if you occasionally spill the communion cup on your new dress or pants.

If you're a soldier who marches with a limp, yet your Commanding Officer orders you to stay on the battlefield, it's for you.

Serve Strong is a book I wrote for myself, and for you, too, if you find it astonishing that God uses you at all.

"If I needed surgery, I would look for the best surgeon I could find. If you need encouragement in serving Christ, you've already found the man who's spent his entire life walking in your shoes. Not only has Terry Powell dedicated his life to service, but he is also uniquely qualified to cogently infuse you with enthusiasm to stay at the task."

—**Jerry B. Jenkins,** novelist and biographer, owner of Christian Writer's Guild

"Terry Powell's book is packed with practical help in maintaining enthusiasm in our walk and work for Christ. *Serve Strong* is a booster shot of encouragement for dragging footsteps, and I commend it to you with pleasure."

—**Rob Morgan,** pastor, Donelson Fellowship, author of over 25 books with 3.5 million in circulation, including *The Red Sea Rules* and the *Then Sings My Soul* series

"Terry's new book on encouragement is truly a cool drink of biblical refreshment for battered spirits. I have struggled my whole life with negative self talk and debilitating feelings of inadequacy. Here is an amazing arsenal of what he calls learning to 'preach to yourself,' in a positive manner. I highly recommend this book to anyone who struggles with discouragement and faces opposition in their life. That should be just about everyone!"

—**Dr. Hans Finzel,** best-selling author of *The Top Ten Mistakes Leaders Make* and anchor of the weekly leadership podcast, *Leadership Answer Man*

"Terry Powell knows the heart of Bible teachers and others involved in ministry. I like his insights. There is great wisdom here. Read it! Enjoy it! Use it!"

—**Murphy Belding,** executive pastor, White River Christian Church, Indianapolis, Indiana

"What refreshing nourishment for the souls of servants! I would love to bless the volunteer staff at the church where I serve with this book. Where can I place my first order to receive this book?"

—**Tim Cox,** family life pastor, Church at Charlotte, Charlotte, North Carolina

"As a leader in a growing global mission organization, I am only too familiar with the opposition, sense of inadequacy, and overwhelming discouragement that derail so many men and women in Christian service. Terry Powell's *Serve Strong* is a powerful, Biblical counterweight to the many forces that drag down God's workers. Its message of encouragement, born out of deep biblical reflection and personal experience, is desperately needed in today's churches and mission fields."

—Steve Richardson, president, Pioneers-USA

"*Serve Strong* is a book that will encourage those who serve and renew their confidence in God's call and leadership. His chapters deal with realistic, practical issues with which those who minister to others struggle, but with powerful Scriptural reminders and personal testimonies that will restore hope and renew the reader."

—Jerry Rankin, president emeritus, International Mission Board, Southern Baptist Convention author, *Spiritual Warfare: The Battle for God's Glory*

"Terry Powell is offering a heart-to-heart talk to his fellow Christian workers. Whether you serve on a volunteer or vocational basis you can really use this counsel and encouragement. Terry knows the rugged landscape of ministry and he refuses to sugarcoat his story or yours. Writing with deep authenticity about struggles and challenges with which we all wrestle, Terry offers Biblical insight that builds hope and courage without indulging in tinny triumphalism. If you're a leader responsible for volunteer or vocational Christian workers, you're going to want to give this book to your co-workers—and keep a well-worn copy close by for yourself."

—Ralph Enlow, president, Association for Biblical Higher Education (ABHE)

"Terry's book will help anyone who serves the Lord, including Sunday School teachers—the world's largest volunteer force! *Serve Strong* will enhance workers' relationship with the Lord, because its solid Bible content will give them a boost and remind them that Christ Himself is their number one asset. It's also written in a conversational, engaging style that will grab and hold readers' attention."

—Marlene Lefever, vice president, David C. Cook, Global, author of *Creative Teaching Methods* and *Learning Styles*

"I enjoyed reading Terry's encouraging, Word-centered perspectives for persons involved in ministry. His personal approach will be helpful to whoever reads this."

—Larry Richards, prolific author of over 200 books, including *Creative Bible Teaching, Zondervan Adventure Bible, Bible Teacher's Commentary,* and *Bible Difficulties Solved*

SERVE
STRONG

SERVE
STRONG

Biblical Encouragement to Sustain God's Servants

TERRY POWELL

LEAFWOOD
PUBLISHERS

SERVE STRONG

Biblical Encouragement to Sustain God's Servants

Copyright 2014 by Terry Powell

ISBN 978-0-89112-432-0
LCCN 2013047972

Printed in the United States of America

Published in association with the Seymour Agency, 475 Miner Street Road, Canton, NY 13617.

LIBRARY OF CONGRESS CATALOGING-IN-PUBLICATION DATA
Powell, Terry.
 Serve strong : biblical encouragement to sustain God's servants / Terry Powell.
   pages cm
 Includes bibliographical references.
 ISBN 978-0-89112-432-0
 1. Perseverance (Ethics)--Biblical teaching. 2. Service (Theology)--Biblical teaching. 3. Christian life--Biblical teaching. I. Title.
   BV4647.P45P69 2014
   248.4--dc23
                                                                  2013047972

Cover design by ThinkPen Design, LLC
Interior text design by Sandy Armstrong

For information contact:
Abilene Christian University Press
1626 Campus Court
Abilene, Texas 79601

1-877-816-4455
www.acupressbooks.com

14 15 16 17 18 19 / 7 6 5 4 3 2 1

To Howard Blomberg

Howard epitomizes the word *friend*.

I've heard him sob over the phone because *I* was hurting. I've watched tears flow down his cheeks because *I* was depressed. When he couldn't personally alleviate my burdens, I've heard him cry out to God on my behalf. When I wasn't sure I could make it through the day, I've known him to leave work just to sit beside me. Few folks have a friend the caliber of Howard.

Because of him, I serve stronger.

CONTENTS

Part Three:
When You Don't See Results

ACKNOWLEDGMENTS

Though writing is a lonely act, it isn't a solo endeavor.

I appreciate my agent, Mary Sue Seymour, for her perseverance in promoting this book; Gary Myers of Leafwood, who saw its potential from the get-go; and my editors at Leafwood, Mary Hardegree and Robyn Burwell, whose expertise assisted in the delivery of the book.

Thanks to my dear friend, Howard Blomberg, who read every word of the manuscript and offered some suggestions that I incorporated. His positive feedback kept me writing when I didn't feel like it.

Thanks to my bride, Dolly, who listened intently as I read aloud first drafts of chapters, and whose eagle-eye rarely misses a typographical error.

I'm grateful for the ladies who typed various chapters from my convoluted, hard-to-decipher handwritten first drafts: Amy Berkley, Sallie Byrd, Anna Donovan, and especially Joyce Hack. Without Joyce's indefatigable efforts during the weeks preceding the deadline, the publisher would still be waiting for the manuscript.

Yet no one deserves more gratitude than my Redeemer, Jesus Christ. When howling winds slam against my boat hurtling waves over the bulwarks, when driving rain pelts the deck and I lose my footing, when ear-piercing thunder rattles the masts and rigging, when lightning bolts cause my heart to lurch . . .

My Anchor holds.

THE ENCOURAGEMENT CONNECTION

MY PLANE LANDED ON THE RUNWAY IN CHARLOTTE, NORTH CAROLINA, AFTER MIDNIGHT. RETURNING FROM an overseas trip, sleep-deprived and physically spent after a week of teaching, my mind was preoccupied with locating my Buick in the remote parking lot and starting the hundred-mile drive home.

I slumped into the driver's seat and turned the key. The car wouldn't start. Not a sound from the crankshaft. No lights. Apparently, when I had removed my luggage from the back seat in the pre-dawn hours a week earlier, I left the interior lights on.

My frustration turned to relief when the shuttle driver who happened by called an airport service vehicle. Soon a pickup pulled alongside my car. The driver connected his working battery to my weak one with jumper cables. The cables served as a conduit, carrying energy from his battery to mine. The next time I turned the key, my engine started and I left for home.

My depleted battery needed an infusion of power from an outside source. Restoring its potential necessitated someone coming alongside and literally making a connection.

Using jumper cables to give someone a jump is an apt analogy for the ministry of encouragement. Life in a fallen world occasionally drains everyone's batteries. Illness, relational strife, unemployment, or susceptibility to temptation depletes resolve and joy. In the sphere of ministry, what siphons off energy may be the adrenalin depletion of excessive commitments, unjust criticism, or doubts about effectiveness. Unless someone replenishes our batteries, we don't make much progress.

What prompted me to write *Serve Strong* is a desire to obey 1 Thessalonians 5:11: "Encourage one another and build up one another." The Greek verb translated "to encourage" literally means "to come alongside" and lend support. That's why the image of jumping a battery fits: encouragement requires that a person come alongside and connect with another, sharing the energy and sustenance he's received from God.

Every Bible passage and truth cited in this book has, at some point over the past four decades, given me a jump. My writing is an attempt to connect with you, to funnel God's truth from my mind and heart to yours.

Recently, someone asked me, "How long does it take to write a book?"

In the case of *Serve Strong*, my unequivocal answer is, "Forty-five years!"

That's how long I've served the Lord in a variety of roles: itinerant Bible teacher, associate church staff member, workshop leader, faculty member at a biblical university, and writer. Time and again, God's Spirit has pulled alongside and infused me with strength through the Bible passages and truths covered in the ensuing chapters.

May these insights that continue to rejuvenate me exert the same effect on you.

Preaching to Yourself

The pastor's six-year-old boy, nestled in his dad's lap on a Sunday afternoon, said,

"Daddy, when you first come out to preach every Sunday, I see you sit there and bow your head. What are you doing that for?"

"I'm asking the Lord to give me a good sermon," his father answered.

"Why don't He?" the boy replied.[1]

Early in his evangelistic preaching ministry, Billy Graham experienced an embarrassing moment prompted by a child's comment. Due to speak at a weekday evening church service in a South Carolina city, Billy needed to mail a letter. During a stroll along a main street, he stopped a boy to ask how to find the post office. After getting the directions, Billy said to the boy, "If you come to the big Baptist Church down the street tonight, I'll tell you how to get to heaven!"

"No thanks," said the boy. "You don't even know how to get to the post office!"[2]

These men told their own stories, confirming the adage that "he who learns to laugh at himself will never cease to be entertained!"

Though preachers are a common butt of jokes and receive their fair share of bad press, anyone serious about following Christ salutes the value of biblical preaching. Sound preaching points listeners to the provision for sin on the cross, instills a God-centered worldview, facilitates godly choices, and enhances love for the Savior. We don't remember the vast majority of sermons we hear. But even ones we've forgotten could have met a need at the time, boosting our spirit during a rough week, informing a decision that was looming, or even surgically removing a cancerous sin pattern from our heart.

Good preaching is like the daily intake of healthy foods and vitamins: the effect is cumulative, over time. One sermon normally doesn't produce spiritual vitality any more than one meal or dose of vitamins radically enhances your health. Yet regular intake results in stronger faith and a healthier walk.

Ask yourself these questions: What's the single most memorable sermon you've ever heard? Why did it leave an indelible impression? Who has been the single most influential preacher for your spiritual pilgrimage?

While the answers to these questions are invaluable, I'm convinced of one particular principle pertaining to the power of sermons—a conviction that permeates my heart, soul, and mind. This is the most life-shaping concept I've experienced this side of the cross:

The most important sermons you'll ever hear aren't the ones faithfully delivered in your church's pulpit (vital as those are to your spiritual health), and they aren't the ones you hear on cable TV or Christian radio stations or CDs. *The most sin-defeating, hope-instilling, faith-sustaining, soul-nourishing, ministry-motivating sermons you'll ever hear are the ones you preach to yourself!*

Talking Back

"Preaching to yourself" is the assertive act of combating discouragement, temptation, or any harmful thought pattern with the truth of Scripture.[3] It's giving a biblically-informed rebuttal to erroneous or distorted thinking.

What and how a follower of Christ thinks, how he "talks to himself," and whether or not he refutes misconceptions and false conclusions is a significant factor affecting spiritual vitality and usefulness to God.

Stuart Briscoe, in a sermon I heard over forty years ago, insisted, "Spiritual experience begins in your mind." He gleaned this conclusion from Romans 12:2: "Do not be conformed to this world, but be transformed by the renewing of your mind." Change in what we feel and how we behave stems from what we think! And we funnel God's truth to our minds by being proactive and talking back to ourselves, not by tolerating the negative self-talk that comes naturally.

The psalms demonstrate the notion of preaching to ourselves. Occasionally, the writers literally talked to themselves about God and their own circumstances. One psalmist talked back to depression by pointing himself to a brighter future stemming from faith in God: "Why are you in despair, O my soul? And *why* have you become disturbed within me? Hope in God, for I shall again praise Him *For* the help of His presence" (Ps. 42:5). In a psalm prompted by an experience of treachery and opposition, David addressed himself concerning God's character: "My soul, wait in silence for God only, For my hope is from Him. He only is my rock and my salvation, My stronghold; I shall not be shaken" (Ps. 62:5–6).

The psalmists often reminded themselves of who God is, what he has done in the past, and what he has pledged to do for his people in the future. They battled unbelief, Satan's lies, and negativism with the weapon of truth, rather than wave a white flag when despair enveloped them.

Sermons for Servants

I'm convinced that cultivating the art of preaching to yourself is a necessary and effective means of applying the remainder of this book. I want you to serve with vigor, to resist urges to quit, to stockpile an arsenal of biblical perspectives to use against threats to your motivation.

I'm all too familiar with the forces that siphon off a Christian worker's passion and hinder effectiveness: physical, mental, and emotional weariness from overwork; feelings of inadequacy for assigned tasks; battle fatigue due to spiritual warfare; failures that inhibit risk-taking; self-imposed inferiority to other leaders; discouragement over apparent lack of fruit; unjust criticism; and second thoughts about the time and financial sacrifices inherent in ministry, to name a few.

What continues to sustain me through more than four decades of vocational ministry is the Holy Spirit's infusion of Scripture that counteracts discouraging things I tell myself, and boosts confidence that God has used and will use me. What you read in *Serve Strong* are biblical messages I've preached to myself—insights that have reassured or invigorated me.

What are the biblical insights about ministry that all of us in God's labor force need to know?

What are the sermons that Christ's servants most need to preach to themselves?

What truths spawn the faith and foster the perseverance needed to keep going as a pastor, missionary, evangelist, Christian school teacher, or behind-the-scenes volunteer?

What Bible verses, when memorized, will come to your rescue at the precise moment you need them?

The remaining pages of *Serve Strong* contain those answers. Are you ready to start *your* sermon preparation?

▬▬▬ Dig Deeper ▬▬▬

What kinds of negative, unbiblical self-talk are you currently experiencing? What does Satan most often whisper in your ear? What effect does this barrage of erroneous input have on your spiritual walk and ministry?

To jumpstart the process of preaching to yourself, memorize Psalm 62:5–6:

> My soul, wait in silence for God only, For my hope is from Him.
> He only is my rock and my salvation, My stronghold; I shall not
> be shaken.

Hiding this God-centered verse in your heart instills raw material for a comforting sermon when you need to rebuff weakness or hopelessness.

Part One

WHEN YOU WONDER
IF IT'S WORTH IT

Serving the Lord involves sacrifice of time and energy, and for some folks, a forfeit of financial security and relational ties. When you wonder if it's worth it, the biblical promises and perspectives in this section will bolster your resolve and fuel endurance.

CHAPTER 1

HE PROMISED HIS PRESENCE

YOU'VE BEEN IN WORSHIP SERVICES WHEN GOD'S SPIRIT LAVISHED ON MEMBERS AN ACUTE AWARENESS OF HIS presence. When choir lyrics or praise team choruses resonated with persons in the pew, prompting spontaneous praise responses. When a reassuring word from Scripture spawned tears that trickled down the cheeks of hurting parishioners. When an overwhelming sense of awe permeated the sanctuary, simulating a "burning bush" experience, convincing folks they were on holy ground.

Or you've preached a sermon or led a Bible study when your zeal spiked and you were absolutely certain God was inspiring your words, and shuttling them from listeners' ears to their hearts.

Perhaps you've engaged unbelievers in conversations when the Holy Spirit prompted you to share a personal anecdote or employ a particular Bible verse that penetrated their defenses.

Perhaps the Holy Spirit has wooed you to intercede for someone, and all through the prayer you remained cognizant of his directing you as if he were whispering in your ear what to say.

The mindfulness of God's presence is a precious experience that nourishes the soul and boosts motivation for ministry.

If only it occurred more often.

To be honest, a deep-rooted consciousness of his presence is more the exception than the rule. Often, we plan, supervise, promote, prepare, teach, witness, recruit, and pray without feeling his nearness at all, just dutifully going through the motions.

For persons heavily involved in ministry, certain situations may engender doubts about the presence of God. When board meetings are rife with tension and mistrust. When disappointment over your grown child's spiritual health siphons off confidence in your calling. When you tap all your wisdom as a counselor, yet couples still break up; when you run on all cylinders for a few weeks, leaving your spirit parched. When persons for whom you're burdened keep rejecting the gospel, or your prayers seem to evaporate before they reach God. These are times when, to use Mark Buchanan's analogy, it seems like God has gone on a long trip and forgot to send a postcard.[1]

When Satan sidles up close and whispers that God has abandoned us, and we're whisker-close to quitting, what biblical perspective can reorient our thinking and foster faith?

What follows isn't complex theology, nor is it an unfamiliar truth to you, but it's a reminder that I regularly preach to myself when a sense of God's presence eludes me.

God with Us

Scripture teems with reminders of a fundamental and reassuring reality: *God is always with his people.* During difficult circumstances, that would be easier to believe if we could see mementos of his presence—the pillar of cloud by day and the pillar of fire by night—as the Israelites in the wilderness did (Exod. 13:21). Without such visible indicators, maintaining rock-ribbed confidence in his nearness requires faith in what his Word says.

What follows are three insights I tell myself when I lose consciousness of his presence.

1. *God himself promised his presence.* The human authors of Scripture didn't merely make the claim. Reassurances of God's presence come from direct quotes attributed to the Lord.

To an afflicted people, he said, "Do not fear, for I am with you; Do not anxiously look about you, for I am your God. I will strengthen you, surely I will help you, Surely I will uphold you with My righteous right hand" (Isa. 41:10). The angel who appeared to Joseph, predicting Jesus' birth, announced, "'And they shall call His name Immanuel,' which translated means, 'God with us'" (Matt. 1:23). The Incarnation was the ultimate evidence of God's direct involvement with his people. After giving a disciple-making mandate to his followers, Jesus added, "And lo, I am with you always, even to the end of the age" (Matt. 28:20). To prepare his inner circle for his physical departure from earth, Jesus assured them, "I will ask the Father, and He will give you another Helper, that He may be with you forever" (John 14:16). Jesus' term for the Holy Spirit was *Paraclete*, literally, "one who comes alongside." It's the noun form of the Greek verb, "to encourage." And the author of Hebrews comforted his readers with these words from the Lord: "I will never desert you, nor will I ever forsake you" (Heb. 13:5).

I recall a year-long span when a shroud of depression enveloped me. Neither prayers nor Bible reading nor medical intervention loosened the vise-grip of despondency. The last thing I was mindful of was the nearness of God. Yet I kept fulfilling my role as professor at a biblical university, striving to remain faithful to my calling.

On one particular day, as I walked across campus to the classroom, an inner voice taunted me. *If God wanted you to teach today, He'd give you the heart for it. Cancel your class and go home. He isn't with you today. When is the last time you felt his presence, anyway!?*

Instantly, God's Spirit projected on the screen of my mind biblical promises I had memorized—the verses I cited earlier. After rehearsing these verses, I addressed myself: *No, I don't feel God's presence today. But his Word, which insists he's with me, is far more reliable than my feelings! I choose to believe he's with me and that he'll enable me to teach, because he said so and he doesn't lie!*

Did my despondent spirit evaporate entirely? No, but those promises buttressed my faith and enabled me to teach passionately that day on the subject matter. Quoting Scripture to myself doesn't magically eradicate problems, yet the discipline sustains me and prompts me to take the next step through the darkness rather than yield to unbelief.

2. *The recipients of God's promised presence were often persons heavily involved in divine tasks.*

When God challenged Moses to go back to Egypt, he said, "I will be with you" (Exod. 3:12). For the fearful, reluctant leader, God added proof of his presence in the form of two miracles: a hand he turned leprous then made whole again, and a rod he transformed into a snake and then back into a rod.

Let's shift to the prophet Jeremiah for the next example. Knowing that he intended decades of difficult tasks and opposition for Jeremiah, the Lord's call included a pledge he could look back on: "Do not be afraid of them, For I am with you to deliver you" (Jer. 1:8).

Moving to the New Testament, Jesus' pledge of his ongoing presence came on the heels of his disciple-making commission (Matt. 28:20). Another reinforcement of divine presence to his work force came near the close of his earthly ministry. His reference to the Holy Spirit's endless companionship as compensation for his upcoming physical absence was for core followers who would keep spreading the gospel after his ascension (John 14:16).

No one understands the stressors and spiritual warfare inherent in ministry more than Jesus. Though the Lord's promised presence encompasses all his people, he especially wants his workers to stay mindful of it.

3. The third anchoring perspective is this: *in Scripture, there is no correlation between the vacillating circumstances of one's ministry and the presence of God.*

No Bible story stokes my awareness of this point better than Joseph's. When traders sold him to Potiphar, an officer in Pharaoh's court, things took a temporary turn for the better. According to Genesis 39:2, "The Lord was with Joseph, so he became a successful man." The next verse adds, "His master saw that the Lord was with him, and *how* the Lord caused all that he did to prosper." Potiphar promoted him making him the overseer of his house in charge of all that he owned.

Then Potiphar's wife falsely accused Joseph of trying to seduce her, resulting in unjust confinement. Though the chief jailor observed natural leadership abilities in Joseph and put him in charge of other prisoners, Joseph wanted out (Gen. 40:14). He accurately interpreted a cellmate's dream, and the chief cupbearer to Pharaoh was restored to his office. Joseph begged him to put in a good word for him before Pharaoh, "Yet the chief cupbearer did not remember Joseph, but forgot him" (Gen 40:23). Two full years passed before the cupbearer told Pharaoh that Joseph could interpret dreams. Only then did Joseph ascend to prominence, second only to Pharaoh, and fulfill God's intended leadership role in light of a coming famine.

When I read Joseph's story, here's what catches my eye: twice in Genesis 39, while Joseph languished in jail, the text announces, "the Lord was with Joseph" (vv. 21, 23). God's presence *before* and *after* Joseph's jail time was no greater than his presence *during* confinement.

Don't let the simplicity of this truth eclipse its significance as you serve. Whether 20 percent more folks attend your church than last year or members are clamoring for your ouster, whether people praise your teaching or you receive letters (unsigned) critical of your views, whether an individual with whom you share the gospel puts her faith in Christ or her heart stays cold and unresponsive, whether you boast a waiting list of Sunday school volunteers or openings persist despite calling every name in the directory, whether you raised the necessary support for the mission field in record time or your departure has been delayed a year for lack of funds, whether you had a ministry position waiting for you as soon as you graduated from seminary or you came up empty after four candidating trips over a two-year span . . .

He's with you.

Ever so slowly, I'm learning to believe that even when I don't feel it.

A Word of Caution

When are the Lord's servants more prone to lose a sense of his presence?

For me, it's after an intense expenditure of time and energy over a short span of time: a teach-all-day-for-a-week summer school course that comes at the close of a demanding semester; a sleep-deprived short-term mission trip; or the implementation of a retreat, conference, or Vacation Bible School that I'm in charge of organizing. Such responsibilities require extra hours and more focused concentration. Put simply, I experience an extended rush of adrenaline that depletes all mental, physical, and emotional reserves.

If this has happened to you, perhaps you, too, felt spiritually dry and emotionally numb for a few days afterward. God seemed more distant. You completed your necessary routine in a more robotic, uninspired manner.

This experience is par for the course for hard-working servants of God! It's similar to what Elijah went through after the emotionally-draining encounter with the prophets of Baal on Mount Carmel. Give yourself permission not to feel for a while. Catch up on your sleep. Don't fret if you're less productive. Plan an activity with family or friends for the sole purpose of having fun.

Please don't misinterpret what's occurring. It isn't a spiritual crisis. Your faith hasn't faltered. God hasn't abandoned you. *Your body is merely collecting its debts.*

Dig Deeper

Bible verses promising God's presence fuel faith when feelings flag. Memorize Isaiah 41:10, Matthew 28:19–20, John 14:16, and Hebrews 13:5.

What effect should belief in God's presence have on us? Find answers in Psalm 16:6, Isaiah 41:10, and Acts 18:9–10.

CHAPTER 2

THE POWER
IS ON!

As a Bible teacher or group facilitator, do you ever lament your lack of formal training, or feel inadequate compared to the abilities of other Bible study leaders you've observed?

As a preacher, have you ever listened to a silver-tongued orator and felt envious because you don't have the same natural capacity to command an audience's attention?

Have you ever observed a Christian worker whose effervescent personality swayed people, all the while wishing you weren't as reserved or introverted?

Who hasn't doubted their usefulness to God based on these criteria!?

But despite the value of training classes or ministerial education . . .

Despite the advantage of exceptional presentation skills dispensed by God's grace to a few choice servants . . .

Despite the magnetic pull of a riveting personality . . .

None of those is the primary factor that gives efficacy to our words as leaders, teachers, and evangelists. The variable that matters most isn't intrinsic to us, nor something we can add to our resume, nor part of our gift mix. It isn't something we work to obtain or that improves with experience. It isn't anything we can take credit for or boast about.

The basis for confidence in our ministries and the key that unlocks fruitfulness is the power inherent in God's Word. No other asset compares to the Holy Spirit's shuttling of Scripture from the ears of listeners to their mind and hearts.

Remind Me Again

I heard of a man who, because of an error during surgery, had the wrong part of his brain removed, totally destroying his memory. In all other areas he functioned well, just without memory. Every time he picked up a newspaper, he read it as if he'd never seen one before. Each time he met someone, it was as if he had never seen the person. Whenever he heard a song, he was for all practical purposes hearing it for the first time. "Relearning" occurred daily.[1]

Despite giving us the capacity for memory, God wants his people to be reminded of certain truths, to relearn them on an ongoing basis. Paul told Titus to remind believers at Crete of particular responsibilities and the core doctrines of salvation, justification, and grace (Tit. 3:1–8). The present imperative verb "remind" in Titus 3:1 suggests repeated action over time.

As someone who serves the Lord, you're familiar with what Scripture says about itself. No doubt you've read and reread verses conveying characteristics of God's Word and why it's integral to Christian living. But if you're like me, when victimized by doubts, inadequacy, or outright lies from Satan about your usefulness, it often seems like part of your brain is missing. We easily forget verses on the Bible's capacity to transform, as well as their implications for our ministries.

We need reminders of the nature of Scripture, to review verses that engender hope concerning our communication of God's Word.

Englisher Samuel Johnson once said, "People more often need to be reminded than instructed."[2]

What follows are two insights about God's Word that I'm constantly relearning.

1. In contrast to our physical bodies or stock market gains, *God's Word is permanent.* What prompts me to engage in the unglamorous task of diligent study of Scripture is awareness that what I write or teach will outlive my years on planet earth.

Peter told his readers that they owed their conversion to God's Word: "You have been born again not of seed which is perishable but imperishable, *that is,* through the living and enduring word of God" (1 Pet. 1:23). Then he added a citation from Isaiah 40: "All flesh is like grass, and all its glory like the flower of grass. The grass withers, and the flower falls off, but the word of the Lord endures forever" (vv. 24–25).

2. *God's Word wields power.* This simple reminder buoys my Spirit when I feel inferior, don't see results, or wonder if all the time and effort invested in Bible teaching is worth it. Memorizing the following verses helps me counteract negative thoughts about the effectiveness of what I do. Just as a believer who's touched by a particular sermon will hear it time and again, preach these verses to yourself over and over when your energy for service needs replenishing.

Jeremiah 23:29. While contrasting his words with those of false prophets, God exclaimed, "Is not My word like fire. . . . and like a hammer which shatters a rock?"

First Thessalonians 2:13. Paul understood that God inspired the words he proclaimed. Reminiscing about his initial preaching venture in Thessalonica, and their responsiveness, he wrote, "We also constantly thank God that when you received the word of God which you heard from us, you accepted *it* not *as* the word of men, but *for* what it really is, the word of God, which also performs its work in you who believe."

Second Timothy 2:9. Though the cost of Paul's ministry included imprisonment, near the end of his life he saw fruitful outcomes from even this adversity. That's why he could write, "but the word of God is not imprisoned."

Hebrews 4:12. When there's no evidence that our communication of Scripture packs a wallop, let's remind ourselves of this assertion: "For the word of God is living and active and sharper than any two-edged sword, and piercing as far as the division of soul and spirit, of both joints and marrow, and able to judge the thoughts and intentions of the heart." Will we believe appearances or our feelings or cling tenaciously to this verse?

A legendary figure from church history revealed the veracity of these verses.

Illustrative Impact

Nineteenth-century British pastor Charles Spurgeon illustrated the transforming effect of God's Word even long after its delivery. He told the story of a pastor named Flavel who felt so burdened about unsaved persons in the congregation that he didn't give the usual benediction after a message. He said to the audience, "How can I dismiss you with a blessing since many of you will be accursed when the Lord returns because you didn't love the Lord Jesus Christ."[3]

Here's how Spurgeon described the outcome for a teenager who was present to hear Flavel's words:

> A lad of fifteen heard that remarkable utterance; and eighty-five years afterwards, sitting under a hedge, I think in Virginia, the whole scene came vividly before him as if it had been but the day before, and it pleased God to bless Mr. Flavel's words to his conversion, and he lived three years longer to bear good testimony that he had felt the power of truth in his heart.[4]

Imagine. Eighty-five years after Flavel shared the gospel and poured out his heart, God's Spirit imprinted his Word onto the heart of the congregant! Time doesn't diminish the potential fruitfulness of a seed faithfully sown. Yet Spurgeon himself discovered that God's Word may exert an immediate influence as well.

In 1867, Spurgeon spoke at a series of meetings in Agricultural Hall, Islington. Remodeling efforts expanded the seating in this vast hall to over eleven thousand. The day before his first message, Spurgeon tested the acoustics of the revamped auditorium, empty at the time, by shouting, "Behold, the Lamb of God, who takes away the sin of the world" (John 1:29). A worker high in the rafters heard him, and as a result converted to faith in Christ.[5]

Personal Evidence

Do you recall the long night a Bible verse or passage comforted you, assuaging your pain?

Can you still see the fog lift on the day a biblical principle clarified which alternative in a career move was better?

Do you remember the battlefield where God's Spirit fortified you against temptation and exposed the lies of Satan through a verse you had memorized?

Can you still see the tears pooling on your carpet and feel the pain piercing your heart from the time God's Word convicted you of sin and spawned repentance?

Then don't lose heart in your ministry! Your own experience with God's Word is all the evidence you need of its clout. What transformed you is the same Word you use when you teach, counsel, or witness. Fuel your faith with the verses in this chapter. Keep reminding yourself of how *you've* experienced the power of Scripture.

Dig Deeper

Digest Psalm 19:7–11. What potential effects of God's Word did David cite?

Take several devotional sessions to read Psalm 119. Pinpoint the values of God's Word, both for you and for those who receive it from you.

CHAPTER 3

BUT
GOD . . .

READ THE WORD IN A LETTER, OR HEAR IT IN A CONVER-
SATION, AND WE CRINGE. WE'RE ON EDGE ABOUT WHAT'S
coming next.

"I really like you, Brad, *but* . . . "

"Susan, you've been a faithful employee for six years, *but* . . . "

"I know I promised we'd get away this weekend, hon, *but* . . . "

"Dad, I know you want me to go to college, *but* . . . "

Shift to the realm of serving the Lord, and the word may have the
same chilling effect.

"I wish I could help out in Sunday School, *but* . . . "

I'm glad that faith makes a difference in your life, *but* . . . "

"Pastor, your idea has merit, *but* . . . "

"You impressed us during the presentation to the Missions
Committee, *but* . . . "

"But" is a conjunction with impact. It precedes a contrary opinion, or introduces a stark contrast to the first part of the sentence. The
term qualifies, alters, or may completely negate what preceded it. In the

examples I provided, "but" kept butting in to reverse the positive direction of the conversation.

Yet we aren't always crestfallen when we read or hear "but." The negative situation may precede this conjunction, with the subsequent content injecting a more optimistic slant. That's especially true in the Bible. There, the first word following a "but" is often "God" or "the Lord," introducing a divine remedy to a discouraging dilemma. A classic case in point is Ephesians 2:1–5. Note the contrast in these selected phrases from this passage: "You were dead in your trespasses and sins.... by nature children of wrath.... *But God*, being rich in mercy ... made us alive together with Christ (by grace you have been saved)" (emphasis mine).

During the mid-twentieth century, V. Raymond Edman, writer of highly regarded devotional books and President of Wheaton College in Illinois, said, "In my devotional reading and study of the Bible, I have come again and again upon the expression 'but God.'"[1] Edman viewed it as a pivot on which hope turned, contrasting our need with God's sufficiency, our weakness or sin with His provision. Verses containing "but God" so nourished his own soul that *But God* became one of his best known devotional books.

Inspired by Edman's affection for the phrase and informed by the book in which he examines thirty-five verses containing it, I've hoisted from God's Word a few "but God" verses brimming with pertinence to Christian workers. Absorb the remainder of this chapter, and you'll never again gloss over "but God" or "but the Lord" in your Bible reading.

From my own pilgrimage, I'll illustrate the efficacy of a particular "but God" passage.

Confidence Booster

I joined the faculty of Columbia International University (then Columbia Bible College) at the ripe old age of thirty-one. The Church Education professor who preceded me was a feisty, strong-willed, creative lady whose students absolutely adored her.

During my first year, I often overheard students praise her or say how they missed her. I felt inferior by comparison. Combine their reverence for her with my own fragile ego, and it's no wonder I felt insecure more often than not. A few times after class, I made a beeline for an unoccupied room in the infirmary, collapsed on the floor, and vented my inadequacies through heartfelt prayer. I figured my predecessor would always eclipse me in their eyes.

I identified with the prophet Jeremiah, who cowered at the prospect of becoming a prophet. In response to God's recruitment of him, he said, "Alas, Lord God. Behold, I do not know how to speak, Because I am a youth" (Jer. 1:6). But his story didn't end with his declaration of inadequacy. The last word belonged to God. The text includes a hinge on which the door opened to a different perspective, shifting the spotlight away from Jeremiah, to the One who called him:

But the LORD said to me,
> "Do not say, 'I am a youth,'
> Because everywhere I send you, you shall go,
> And all that I command you, you shall speak.

"Do not be afraid of them,
> For I am with you to deliver you," declares the Lord.

Then the Lord stretched out His hand and touched my mouth,
and the Lord said to me,
> "Behold, I have put My words in your mouth." (Jer. 1:7–9, emphasis mine)

To say that Jeremiah's prophetic ministry taxed him is an understatement. Ridicule, persecution, and rejection were his lot. Yet God's enablement propelled him into four decades of faithfulness as God's spokesman.

Jeremiah's brittle confidence, contrasted with God's pledge of his presence, resonated with me. God's Spirit branded this "but the Lord" story on my mind, instilling my own persistence as a professor. As of this book's release date, I'm finishing thirty-three years on the faculty. The only explanation for my longevity is "but the Lord." He equipped me for what he called me to do.

When *you* don't feel up to tackling God's assignment, anchor your thoughts in the deep waters of Jeremiah 1:4–9.

Yes, But . . .

From a list of over fifty "but God" references, I've cherry-picked eight more with relevance to ministry involvement. The left column identifies a felt need or a threatening circumstance. The right side counters with a verse containing the conjunction that makes all the difference. The boldfaced words represent my emphasis, not that of biblical authors.

I'm drained physically and despondent in spirit. My resolve to keep going is waning.	"My flesh and my heart fail, **but God** is the strength of my heart, and my portion forever" (Ps. 73:26).
My critics are relentless. They're out to destroy me.	In response to threats from an adversary, David wrote, "**But You, O Lord**, are a shield about me, My glory, and the One who lifts my head" (Ps. 3:3).
Their treatment of me isn't fair. They're sinning against me.	Joseph immersed himself in the sovereignty of God, telling his brothers who had sold him into slavery, "You meant evil against me, **but God** meant it for good in order to bring about this present result, to preserve many people alive" (Gen. 50:20).
I've pushed hard for so long that I've depleted my adrenalin and emotional reserves. Now there's little motivation for the daily routine. It's been a long time since I felt this despondent.	Paul could identify! "When we came into Macedonia our flesh had no rest, but we were afflicted on every side: conflicts without, fears within. **But God**, who comforts the depressed, comforted us by the coming of Titus" (2 Cor. 7:5–6).

I thought personal purity would get easier with age, but the longer I serve the Lord, the more temptations to sin bombard me. Satan never takes a break in his efforts to derail me. Sometimes I grow weary of the battle and want to give in.	"**But the Lord** is faithful, and He will strengthen and protect you from the evil *one*" (2 Thess. 3:3).
I don't feel qualified for the task God assigned me. My feelings of inadequacy sap my joy. I just don't have what it takes.	In response to critics trying to undermine Paul's ministry in Corinth, he told church members that their conversion to Christ was the evidence of his credibility as an apostle (2 Cor. 3:1–4). Then he shifted the spotlight from himself to the Lord, who had enabled him to succeed. Notice the contrast: "Not that we are adequate in ourselves to consider anything as *coming* from ourselves, **but our adequacy is from God**, who also made us adequate as servants of a new covenant" (2 Cor. 3:5–6).
I put a lot of pressure on myself to succeed. When there's little to show for my efforts, frustration envelopes me.	Paul suggested that ministry outcomes aren't our responsibility. When a contentious spirit surfaced in Corinth over allegiance to different leaders, Paul wrote, "I planted, Apollos waters, **but God** was causing the growth. So then neither the one who plants nor the one who waters is anything, **but God** who causes the growth" (1 Cor. 3:6–7).

With which need do you most identify right now? Open your Bible to the corresponding passage and read it again in an unhurried manner.

Prayer Partners

I've saved the best for last.

The capstone of this chapter is a "but" spoken by Jesus to Peter in reference to spiritual warfare. Jesus didn't soft-pedal the inevitability of opposition and struggle for those who serve him. He even intimated that Peter would let him down: "Simon, Simon, behold, Satan has demanded *permission* to sift you like wheat; *but I have prayed for you*, that your faith may not fail; and you, when once you have turned again, strengthen your brothers" (Luke 22:31–32, emphasis mine).

Jesus' pledge of intercession for Peter extends to all of his followers. After his resurrection and ascension, Jesus launched a ministry of prayer for his people: "Christ Jesus is He who died, yes, rather who was raised, who is at the right hand of God, *who intercedes for us*" (Rom. 8:34, emphasis mine).

God the Son isn't the only member of the Trinity who's praying for us. The Holy Spirit complements Jesus' intercession: "In the same way the Spirit also helps our weakness; for we do not know how to pray as we should, but the Spirit Himself intercedes for *us* with groaning too deep for words; and He who searches the hearts knows what the mind of the Spirit is, because He intercedes for the saints according to *the will of* God" (Rom. 8:26–27).

Keep asking others in the body of Christ to pray for your teaching, for God's Spirit to shuttle truth from the heads of learners to their hearts. Keep inviting them to plead with God that the filters of unbelievers are removed so that they will be receptive to the message of the gospel as you share it. Don't stop soliciting prayers for the tough decisions on the agenda for the next board meeting. But remember that Jesus Christ and the Holy Spirit are already interceding on your behalf!

There's that "but" again.

Dig Deeper

Memorize Psalm 73:26: "My flesh and my heart may fail; but God is the strength of my heart and my portion forever."

John Piper emphasizes the significance of this verse in battling discouragement:

> Literally the verb is simply, "My flesh and my heart fail!" I am despondent! I am discouraged! But then immediately he fires a broadside against his despondency: "But God is the strength of my heart and my portion forever."

The psalmist does not yield. He battles unbelief with counterattack.[2]

Find a copy of Edman's *But God* online and digest its thirty-five short chapters. You'll find verses highlighting God's mercy, his promise to meet material needs, Jesus' resurrection, and much more.

CHAPTER 4

NETLESS FOLLOWERS

WHAT IS A "NETLESS CHRISTIAN"?

———————

As soon as Dave finished seminary and they raised enough support, he and his wife, Jeannie, left with their three young sons for a mission post thousands of miles away. No longer were their parents close by to dote on their boys. No longer could they text intimate friends and meet them at Panera Bread for coffee. No longer could they run to a nearby Kroger for a missing food item. Their excitement of fulfilling Christ's call to go to an area unreached by the gospel was tempered by the loss of companionship and a familiar routine.

———————

The Sanfords experienced netlessness at a later stage in life. Still healthy at retirement in their mid-sixties, they took classes in TEFL (Teaching English as a Foreign Language), then accepted a two-year teaching stint in a Muslim country. Though unable to proselytize openly as Christians, their intent was to share their faith informally through relationships they established. They left behind a twenty-five-year affiliation with a local church where they knew almost everyone, three grown children within a two-hour drive, plus five grandkids—and a sixth on the way. Their departure was bittersweet, yet they were convinced it was what Christ wanted them to do.

The nets Bruce abandoned in his mid-forties included an executive position at a bank, with an escalating salary that guaranteed a lifetime of financial security if he stayed a few more years. But he felt the Lord's tug on his heart for the pastorate. Obedience required an out-of-state move to Bible college, then three additional years in seminary.

When he announced his resignation to an associate at the bank, the other officer lamented that Bruce had "gone off the deep end." The associate recommended a professional counselor who could get Bruce and his wife back on track. Bruce's father, a Christian, shook his head and muttered, "I can't believe that you're doing what you're doing! You just don't leave such a good-paying job." And stunned at what she considered a ludicrous career decision, Bruce's mother-in-law hardly spoke to him for a year. Yet for Bruce and Kim, Christ's call to serve the local church was nonnegotiable. A dozen years later, he's ensconced as pastor of a midwestern church.

Net-Dropping Disciples

The idea of a netless follower of Christ stems from Jesus' call of four disciples in Matthew 4:18–22. As you read, lock your mental lens on what they discarded or left behind:

> Now as Jesus was walking by the Sea of Galilee, He saw two brothers, Simon who was called Peter, and Andrew his brother, casting a net into the sea; for they were fishermen. And He said to them, "Follow Me, and I will make you fishers of men." Immediately they left their nets and followed Him. Going

on from there He saw two other brothers, James the son of Zebedee, and John his brother, in the boat with Zebedee their father, mending their nets; and He called them. Immediately they left the boat and their father, and followed Him.

Their nets represented the only vocation they had ever known. Following Christ meant the loss of a regular income and a seismic shift in daily routine. Becoming "fishers of men" also involved detaching themselves, at least for a while, from family members. Joseph Stowell elaborates on the effects of their decision: "Their career provided security, significance, position . . . income, and, in some regard, meaning to life. This was a high-risk, high-sacrifice step. But what is amazing is that all of them immediately left that which hindered them from being followers and stepped out to follow Him."[1]

My primary aim in this chapter isn't to promote such radical discipleship; it's to encourage those of you who've already dropped nets to heed Christ's summons to serve. Like the disciples, as well as the persons cited in the beginning of this chapter, you're already a committed follower who has sacrificed material affluence, cherished customs, leisure pursuits, or companionship of friends and family. Chances are, if you could do it over again, you'd ratify your original decision to serve Christ despite the costs. You've seen him use you in others' lives and you know the deep-seated joy of being in God's will and experiencing his favor.

But for some netless servants, hardships generate doubts about their particular ministry calling. Unresponsiveness of people, physical challenges, financial stress, criticism, or outright spiritual warfare may cause niggling thoughts to surface that second-guess a prior commitment.

If you ever long for the security and comfort of nets you left behind, fixate on the promise of the One who said "Follow Me!" in the first place. An examination of this promise suggests that you aren't sacrificing as much as you thought.

Bountiful Compensation

Jesus imparted the promise I'm referring to long after his initial call of the twelve disciples. In the verses preceding the promise, a wealthy young man refused to sell his possessions and turned his back on Christ. Our Lord pointed out how difficult it is for a rich person to enter the kingdom of God. That's when Peter butted in. To spotlight the contrast between the core disciples and the rich man, Peter exclaimed, "Behold, we have left everything and followed you" (Mark 10:28).

Set your scope on Jesus' reply:

> Truly I say to you, there is no one who has left house or brothers or sisters or mother or father or children or farms, for My sake and for the gospel's sake, but that he will receive a hundred times as much now in the present age, houses and brothers and sisters and mothers and children and farms, along with persecutions; and in the age to come, eternal life. (vv. 29–30)

Jesus acknowledged that heeding his call may involve dropping the nets of family ties, personal residence, and vocation. Then he put such sacrifices in proper perspective, pledging a hundredfold return in this realm of time and space, as well as the benefit of eternal life.

Clearly, Jesus didn't mean we'll literally get back a hundred times the income we forfeited or that we'll eventually reside in a mansion that dwarfs the apartment or house we were in at the time of our call. The verses preceding this promise illustrate how a materialistic mindset hinders radical discipleship, mandating a non-literal interpretation of Jesus' words. Any speaker who wields this promise to manipulate people to give to *their* ministry, just so the giver will get back even more, is giving a convenient, carnal interpretation. The incredulous claim of the "prosperity gospel" is also negated by Jesus' reference to persecution as part of the package. Besides, who needs a hundred houses, and who could get along with a hundred times the number of siblings and parents?!

Yet Jesus *is* pledging manifold blessings in the here and now to counter what we've waived in order to follow him. Perhaps he's alluding to relationships in the extended family of God; or to the sheer contentment of knowing our lives count for eternity. I've enjoyed the privilege of traveling overseas twenty-five times to train national church workers. The financial costs, energy depletion, and bouts of spiritual warfare were more than compensated for by the hundreds of new brothers and sisters I now have in places like Ukraine, India, Sri Lanka, and Kenya. And joy permeates my heart, knowing I'm contributing to the cause that will outlive my earthly body.

Yet in John Piper's view, it's *Christ himself* who offsets every sacrifice. Here's his commentary on Mark 10:29–30:

> If you give up a mother's nearby affection and concern, you get back one hundred times the affection and concern from the ever-present Christ. If you give up the warm comradeship of a brother, you get back one hundred times the warmth and comradeship of Christ. If you give up the sense of at-homeness you had in your house, you get back one hundred times the comfort and security of knowing that the Lord owns every house and land and stream and tree on earth.[2]

Piper continues, addressing prospective missionaries with these words: "Jesus says, 'I promise to *work* for and *be* for you so much that you will not be able to speak of having sacrificed anything.'"[3] To illustrate the escalation of intimacy with Christ for those who sacrificially serve him, Piper tells the story of John G. Paton, missionary to the New Hebrides (today's Vanuatu in the South Pacific). Paton testified to the precious nearness of Christ when he felt utterly alone, having lost his wife and child, surrounded by hostile natives as he hid in a tree.

> I climbed into the tree and was left there alone in the bush. The hours I spent there live all before me as if it were but of

yesterday. I heard the frequent discharging of muskets, and the yells of the Savages. Yet I sat there among the branches, as safe in the arms of Jesus. Never, in all my sorrows, did my Lord draw nearer to me, and speak more soothingly in my soul, than when the moonlight flickered among these chestnut leaves, and the night air played on my throbbing brow, as I told all my heart to Jesus. Alone, yet not alone! If it be to glorify my God, I will not grudge to spend many nights alone in such a tree, to feel again my Savior's spiritual presence, to enjoy His consoling fellowship.[4]

Jesus' reply to Peter's declaration of self-denial was in essence a rebuke, not a commendation. How could Peter consider the nets he abandoned a sacrifice in light of increased intimacy with Christ, and the other-worldly value of employment in God's redemptive program?

An exceptional women's Bible study leader cut back to half-time employment so she could study more for her volunteer teaching engagements. She could use the income she relinquished. But the money can't compare to the charge she gets when young women under her tutelage start delving into and falling in love with God's Word. One "Aha!" moment, when a group member's smile radiates from ear to ear because she grasps a principle, blesses her far more than a pricier vacation ever could.

Bruce also confirms that Jesus keeps his promise of blessing for persons who leave behind their nets. He's the ex-banker you met early in this chapter who left a flourishing career to train for the pastorate. After six years at a church, he says there's no greater thrill than leading a young man to Christ, later officiating at his wedding, and subsequently baptizing his first child. No financial security or esteem in the business world could match his unbridled joy of seeing over a hundred persons respond to an altar call, a few praying to receive Christ, the majority confessing sin and getting right with God and with each other through tears.

Bruce validates God's call to the marketplace for some people, but in his case, he's grateful for an infinitely greater reason to get up in the morning.

Dig Deeper

Think of an individual or couple who "dropped nets" in order to serve Christ. Perhaps following Christ's call moved them an ocean apart from family and friends. Perhaps this church staff member forfeited material security to heed the Lord's summons later in life. Write this individual or couple a hand-written letter, expressing gratitude for their ministry, and identifying any way in which you've personally benefited from service they've rendered. In your note, employ Jesus' promise in Mark 10:29–30 as a means of encouragement.

CHAPTER 5

A Pebble in the Pond

You've seen the *ripple effect*.

Toss a pebble into a pond. Tiny waves, forming concentric circles, roll outward from the point of impact until they become too small to see.

Figuratively speaking, the ripple effect refers to the gradual, long-range consequences of a spoken word, deed, or event. A chain of causation begins with the original agent, setting in motion a process of influence. One individual inspires another resulting in that person's impact on a third party who in turn affects someone else. The upshot of it all is that our lives have more sway than we think.

That's especially true in the realm of ministry. Whether you communicate God's Word, recruit others to teach, plan a life-altering youth retreat, lead a neighbor to Christ, or give toward a missionary's support, what you do produces waves of grace that keep expanding—all the way to eternity!

Rivet this perspective deep into your consciousness and keep preaching it to yourself: your potential for Christ isn't limited to the Bible lessons *you* teach, to the people *you* lead to faith in Christ, to the ministries *you* pioneer, or to the values *you* model before others. Your potential isn't hemmed in by the extent of *your* own abilities. *Your potential includes the future contributions for Christ of whomever you influence, plus those of persons they in turn inspire or serve, and so on, ad infinitum.* When it comes to intellect, giftedness, or opportunity, others may run proverbial circles around you. Yet something *you* said or did affected them, becoming the pebble that fell into the water.

The life of Barnabas illustrates the ripple effect in relation to ministry and epitomizes this expanded understanding of your potential.

What's in a Name?

Imagine folks at your church started calling you by a new name that reflected your character. Such a moniker could either affirm or devastate you, depending on how you've behaved.

That's what happened to a member of the very first local church in Jerusalem. Leaders of the congregation scuttled his given name, Joseph, and tagged him with "Barnabas," which means "Son of Encouragement." What prompted the name change? What did he say and do that left such a favorable impression? Before observing the long-range effect of Barnabas' life, let's identify whom he encouraged, and how.

Church of Jerusalem
Acts 4:32–37

This local assembly launched with three thousand members who came to Christ after Peter's sermon on the Day of Pentecost (Acts 2:37–41). Before long, tension surfaced between the converts and Jews who didn't view Jesus as the Messiah. Some unbelievers boycotted the shops and kiosks owned by Christians, resulting in financial hardship. This ostracism, combined with the rapidly escalating number of believers, caused an ever-widening discrepancy between the haves and have-nots within the church.

Well-to-do members sold properties and gave the funds to church leaders to distribute (Acts 2:45; 4:34–35). The only person singled out for his giving was Barnabas, "who owned a tract of land, sold it and brought the money and laid it at the apostles' feet" (Acts 4:37). The reference to his name change in this context suggests that such unselfishness on Barnabas' part was a pattern, not an isolated incident. Acts 4:33 shows the effects of this expression of authentic fellowship: "And with great power the apostles were giving witness to the resurrection of the Lord Jesus, and abundant grace was upon them all."

By releasing his resources, exhibiting a "God's property" mindset toward his possessions, Barnabas encouraged the needy as well as the leaders who felt responsible for the members' welfare.

Plunk. A pebble smashes into the surface of the pond.

Saul
Acts 9:26–28

A zealous Pharisee, Saul was a ringleader in the persecution of the church that began with the stoning of Stephen. He breathed "threats and murder against the disciples of the Lord" (Acts 9:1). After Christ miraculously appeared to Saul on the road to Damascus, his life did an about-face. With a fervent spirit, he began proclaiming Jesus as the Son of God in the synagogues of Damascus.

Returning to Jerusalem, Saul encountered an obstacle to the pursuit of his new calling: believers there "were all afraid of him, not believing that he was a disciple" (Acts 9:26). They couldn't get past his previous staunch opposition to the gospel, wondering if his conversion story was a ploy to destroy the church from within.

Next comes a hinge verse on which the progress of the gospel turned: "*But Barnabas* took hold of him and brought him to the apostles and described to them how he had seen the Lord on the road . . . and how at Damascus he had spoken out boldly in the name of Jesus" (Acts 9:27, emphasis mine). The leaders heeded Barnabas' intervention, for Saul (later Paul) "was moving about freely in Jerusalem, speaking out boldly in the name of the Lord" (Acts 9:28).

With a timely word, Barnabas defended Paul's testimony and sponsored him among the leaders in Jerusalem.

Plop. Another small stone slaps the surface of the pond.

Converts in Antioch, Paul
Acts 11:19–26

A martyr's blood became the seed for the planting of new congregations. Those who fled Jerusalem after the death of Stephen shared the gospel wherever they went, including the Gentile-saturated city of Antioch. When news of mass conversions reached Jerusalem, leaders sent Barnabas to guide the infant church.

Exhibiting a positive spirit, Barnabas acknowledged God's grace among them. He modeled a Spirit-filled, trusting life and urged them to stick with their commitment to Christ. Knowing the task of nurturing them exceeded his limits, Barnabas took a recruiting trip to Tarsus, where Paul had been exiled after Jewish antagonists threatened his life in Jerusalem (Acts 9:29–30). Having observed Paul's penchant for proclamation, he brought him back to Antioch, where for a year they both followed up the decisions for Christ through teaching. Ever-increasing numbers put their faith in Christ.

Through his optimistic presence, spoken words of reassurance, and gift of teaching, Barnabas stabilized new believers who had shucked their pagan background. Barnabas also yanked Paul out of seclusion, providing him a venue for service and propelling a public ministry that would far eclipse his own.

Plunk. Plunk. Two pebbles simultaneously smack the water.

John Mark
Acts 15:35–41

Barnabas' younger cousin assisted him and Paul during part of their first church-planting venture (Acts 13–14). Early in the campaign, Mark deserted them, preferring the comforts of his home in Jerusalem to the rigors of pioneer work in hostile environments (Acts 13:13). Despite life-threatening opposition, Paul and Barnabas kept preaching in various cities throughout Syria and Cilicia, convincing many to put their faith in Christ. Eventually, they returned to their sending church in Antioch, then gained an audience before leaders in Jerusalem, where they reported on God's grace among the Gentiles.

When Paul broached the idea of a follow-up visit to the churches they had established, Barnabas wanted Mark to accompany them again. Paul adamantly resisted, citing Mark's previous abandonment. A contentious argument ensued, causing a rift between the leaders. Paul replaced Barnabas with Silas. Barnabas put his arm around Mark and left for more obscure ministry in Cyprus.

By standing up for him before Paul and through being a physical presence while Mark's faith developed roots, Barnabas cultivated within Mark a hope for usefulness in the cause for Christ.

Splash. Ever-expanding undulations in the water move farther and farther from the point of impact.

*For a more thorough treatment of John Mark's story, see chapter thirteen, "Failure Is Not Final."

Dramatic Impact

Keep in mind that one's ministry potential encompasses all the accomplishments of people whom we reach or influence. Things we say and do become small stones dropping into the pond, causing a chain reaction of effects for eternity. Nobody's story in the Bible demonstrates this phenomenon better than Barnabas'.

In Jerusalem, his giving buoyed the spirits of destitute converts and alleviated pressure on the leaders of this burgeoning congregation. The proceeds given by men such as Barnabas freed the twelve apostles to evangelize and to teach. They could invest in more hands-on ministry to members since they didn't have to scrounge around for paying jobs.

The ultimate outcome of such sacrificial devotion was the spread of the gospel to new geographical areas. Members who had been discipled in Jerusalem, forced to flee after Stephen's martyrdom, witnessed for Christ wherever they went. The waves rolled all the way to Samaria, Phoenicia, Cyprus, and Antioch (Acts 8:4–5; 11:19).

On two pivotal occasions, Barnabas intervened for Paul, defending him before suspicious leaders in Jerusalem and recruiting him to help with the nurture of converts in Antioch. The achievements eventually listed in Paul's obituary far outstripped the copy in Barnabas': church planter, author of a sizeable chunk of Scripture, and outside of Christ himself, the most prominent figure in the New Testament. But without Barnabas, would any of us even know Paul's name?

Barnabas' encouragement and discipleship of new believers in Antioch also caused ripples. There, followers of Jesus were first called "Christians" and Antioch became the first missionary-sending congregation. After an intense bout of prayer and fasting, Spirit-guided leaders whom Barnabas and Paul had trained dispatched them to unreached areas (Acts 13:1–4).

Perhaps the most eye-opening example of Barnabas' long-term impact involved John Mark. After years of silence, Mark showed up in Rome as Peter's assistant (1 Pet. 5:13). Paul's own attitude toward Mark shifted dramatically. Twice he cited Mark as a fellow worker (Col. 4:10; Phil. 24). While incarcerated in Rome with only months to live, Paul urged Timothy, "Pick up Mark and bring him with you, for he is useful to me for service" (2 Tim. 4:11). Mark's primary legacy is the Gospel that bears his name: a fast-paced narrative that Bible translators often use to introduce unreached people to Christ.

Mark's early desertion of Paul and Barnabas demonstrated immaturity and lack of readiness for frontline ministry. But working with people is like mining for gold: there's lots of dirt to sift through, but we aren't looking for the dirt. Barnabas saw a mother lode of potential in Mark, and he made a sacrificial decision to excavate it. God still woos people to himself through the writings of a failure, to whom Barnabas gave a fresh chance to serve.

So What?

Do you ever feel a tinge of envy toward someone in ministry whose platform for influence is much larger and sturdier than yours? Look for a chance to encourage this person. Intercede regularly for him or her so the waves this person creates extend farther than they would have without you.

Do you ever wish you had a spiritual gift or ability that God didn't give you? Pray for an opportunity to lead to Christ someone who'll have such a capacity for service. What counts isn't whether you do it, but whether you inspire or enable the person who *can* accomplish it.

Have you concluded that your weaknesses outnumber your strengths, vastly diminishing your usefulness? Do you figure that your competencies are so few and far between that the only things you have to offer others are your time, physical presence, and a few words of reassurance?

Then never underestimate what God will do through *you*, knowing what he did through Barnabas and through the people he encouraged.

Plop. Dive into the pond and trust God for ripples to extend farther than your eye can see.

Dig Deeper

In this chapter I highlighted one theme in the life of Barnabas: the long-range results of what he said and did in relation to two churches and two colleagues. For a more comprehensive study of the four episodes that feature him (Acts 4:32–37; 9:26–28; 11:19–26; 15:35–41), mull over these questions:

What impresses you most about Barnabas? Why?

What did Barnabas say and do to earn the title "Son of Encouragement"?

What character traits did he exhibit?

Why are those particular traits essential for a ministry of encouragement?

Who has been a "Barnabas" in relation to you? What has this person said or done to help you?

Who in your sphere of influence could use a word or act of encouragement from you this week? What is God's Spirit nudging you to say to this person or to do for him or her?

CHAPTER 6

PLAYING BACK GOD'S CALL

THE YEAR I TURNED THIRTY-SIX, MY SONS STOOD ON THE PRECIPICE OF ADOLESCENCE. I LOOKED AHEAD SIX YEARS— knowing they would pass with the speed of light—to when my older boy would enter college. Questions about the affordability of their college education nagged me. On a Bible-college salary, I couldn't fulfill a pledge I had made to pay half the costs. My wife's part-time job helped make ends meet, but substantial savings weren't feasible.

At the same time, a heartfelt yearning churned inside me for a more authentic walk with the Lord. Since my late teens, all I had known vocationally was some form of Christian service. Sometimes I felt like a "professional Christian" who met role expectations, rather than someone who enjoyed an intimate, soul-satisfying relationship with the Lord. I wondered if I loved the Lord's work more than I loved *him*.

Repeatedly, these questions goaded me: If I weren't "paid to be a Christian," would I follow Christ wholeheartedly? If I didn't receive income to teach it, would I carve out time for God's Word? Could I thrive relationally in an environment that didn't consist entirely of Christians?

If I earned my paycheck in the marketplace, would zeal for the Lord and for his redemptive work still consume me? I wasn't sure I could say yes to those questions.

My challenging monetary situation worked in tandem with questions about my identity to inspire an intriguing possibility: should I resign from the faculty and launch a career in business? The move would address both felt needs in one swoop: improving finances and testing the genuineness of my faith. For months I prayed about the idea, even jotting down names of contacts who might recommend or sponsor me for a different line of work.

But as I write this, I'm completing my thirty-second consecutive year as a full-time faculty member at Columbia International University. Back in 1986, the more I thought and prayed about it, the more convinced I became that God intended for me to stay. He calls many men and women to the marketplace, but I wasn't one of them.

What convinced me to recommit to my role as a professor and instilled persistence in me for this ministry? What kept me from roaming in greener financial pastures?

A specific biblical insight informed my decision. This perspective can engender sticktoitiveness within you for your own sphere of service. Whether you're a pastor, missionary, a Sunday school teacher, or someone God *has* called to the marketplace, grasping this principle will cultivate endurance when you're weary, when you face daunting opposition, when you're not seeing the desired results, or even when it's hard to make it on your salary.

Hearing God's Call

When you assumed your current ministry responsibility, you didn't treat the decision glibly. Especially if it's the way you earn a living, with all that was at stake, you undoubtedly asked God for wisdom, solicited others' prayers, weighed the job description in light of your strengths and weaknesses, and invited others' input. You utilized objective information to reach a subjective, yet convincing, conclusion: *God is leading me to accept.*

Here's the insight that swayed my thinking twenty-seven years ago. It's why I didn't resign and start over in a new venture. *Awareness that God called us to a specific ministry and led us to accept a particular venue of service fuels perseverance. Believing we are currently where he once put us makes us hesitant to leave and keeps us from bailing out when the going gets rough.*

In the next several pages, I'll glean examples of this principle from Scripture and illustrate it from outside the domain of vocational ministry.

Biblical Examples

God's method of recruiting workers varied with the individual. To convince Moses that he wanted him to break the yoke of Egyptian bondage on his chosen people, God spoke through a burning bush (Exod. 3). When Pharaoh kept resisting and when the Israelites kept grumbling about provisions in the wilderness, did the unmistakable nature of God's call nourish Moses' resolve?

An angelic visitor informed Gideon that he'd free his people from the vise grip of the Midianites (Judg. 6). Did this intervention from heaven instill confidence within Gideon when he faced long odds against his foes?

During the years he spent dodging Saul's spears, did David receive inspiration from the memory of Samuel's anointing him as the next king (1 Sam. 16)?

What propped up Jeremiah during four decades of difficult ministry? What kept him going when the people he tried to reach taunted him, dropped him into a slimy pit, and burned the only written version of his prophecy? Was it the following words of God's call, seared forever on his memory? "Before you were born I consecrated you; I have appointed you a prophet to the nations. . . . I have put My words in your mouth" (Jer. 1:5, 9).

Perhaps Paul offers the most incisive example of persistence fueled by awareness of God's call. His apostolic career was fraught with obstacles and persecution. Notice the afflictions cited in 2 Corinthians 11:24–28:

> Five times I received from the Jews thirty-nine *lashes*. Three times I was beaten with rods, once I was stoned, three times I was shipwrecked, a night and a day I have spent in the deep. *I have been* on frequent journeys, in dangers from rivers, dangers from robbers, dangers from *my* countrymen, dangers from the Gentiles, dangers in the city, dangers in the wilderness, dangers on the sea, dangers among false brethren; *I have been* in labor and hardship, through many sleepless nights, in hunger and thirst, often without food, in cold and exposure. Apart from *such* external things, there is the daily pressure on me *of* concern for all the churches.

His summons to preach the gospel came simultaneously with his conversion on the road to Damascus. The same Christ who stopped Paul in his tracks told him, "For this purpose I have appeared to you, to appoint you a minister and a witness not only to the things you have seen, but also to the things in which I will appear to you" (Acts 26:16).

In Paul's own references to his divine commission, he emphasized the same factor that stitched together the Old Testament stories I cited: *God's initiative*. In the greeting of his letter to the Galatians, he called himself an apostle "not *sent* from men nor through the agency of man, but through Jesus Christ" (Gal. 1:1). In other letters, he insisted that he was an apostle "by the will of God" or "according to the commandment of God" (Eph. 1:1; Col. 1:1; 1 Tim. 1:1). Persecution and deprivation didn't deter him because he knew he carried out *God's* wishes. He didn't concoct his assignment in his own mind.

Paul's use of the passive voice in relation to his calling reinforces this perspective. (Passive voice indicates that the subject is the recipient of an action, not the originator of what transpires. He's acted upon by an outside agent.) In 1 Timothy 1:11 and Titus 1:3, he mentioned the gospel message "with which I have been [or was] entrusted."

To maintain that a realization of God's calling enabled Paul to endure isn't a stretch. Why else would he repeatedly refer to the nature of his appointment as an apostle?

Now let's apply the principle to God's guidance of his servants in the twenty-first century.

How God Leads

Unless I miss my guess, you're thinking that there's a vast difference between the way God called biblical characters and his typical approach to guiding folks today.

That's correct. Most likely, he didn't lead you to your church staff position, to a specific mission field, to teach first-graders in Sunday school, or to start a business through a miraculous manifestation, an angelic visitor, or an out-of-the-blue audible voice from heaven. For us, discerning God's will is more of a process, and it's a whole lot more subjective. The degree of certainty may not be as high.

Yet the difference in the means God employs doesn't invalidate the principle: *knowing he led us to a sphere of service cultivates the endurance needed to fulfill that ministry.*

Instead of getting our attention through a supernatural phenomenon, God discloses a need he wants us to meet by speaking to us during a sermon or personal Bible study. Instead of intervening through the incarnation of an angel, he directs us through a church leader who confirms a spiritual gift and offers a venue for exercising it. Instead of an ear-splitting voice that comes out of nowhere, we "hear" the silent, yet unmistakable whisper of God's Spirit after an intense round of prayers for wisdom or through the counsel of a godly friend. A method or process of recruitment that's less spectacular doesn't negate the fact that God still speaks and directs his people to particular venues for a redemptive purpose.

The scope of this chapter's applicability is broader than vocational Christian workers or church volunteers. Though he didn't give me a green light to enter the business world, he plants others in the marketplace for the purpose of growing his kingdom. Or perhaps you're someone he has guided to a particular college or seminary to prepare for a vocation he's chosen for you. In those situations, remembering his leading will stimulate your best effort and sustain you through uninspired days.

I'm not saying that God never revises his plans for us. Now and then he gives a new assignment, involving a different position or type of service. Yet if we're convinced he put us where we are, we're less likely to make an impulsive decision that we later regret. We initially resist the lure of a change, especially if the new opportunity looks more attractive because of challenges in our current position. We're open to God moving us elsewhere, but we're committed to the role he previously assigned until he makes it crystal clear he's redirecting us.

When I'm tempted to quit or lured by a new opportunity, here's how I apply this concept to my prayers: "Father, I know without a doubt that You led me to my current position. But I'm not sure that You're calling me to leave it. I don't know if I can trust my motives. But I do trust You, and if You want to move me, I'm relying on You to provide the same degree of certitude regarding a change that I had when I accepted my current role. I'm willing to obey You, but I'm resolved to stay where You put me until I know it's You who's moving me."

From the pages of history, I've culled an epic story of how awareness of God's call fosters endurance. And it's from the realm of politics.

A Model of Persistence

In the late 1700s, the British economy relied heavily on the slave trade from Africa. Most captives toiled on large plantations owned by Britishers in the West Indies. The annual export of slaves from Africa's western coast exceeded one hundred thousand.

A year after converting to Christ, William Wilberforce (1759–1833), a member of Parliament, sensed a call on his life that would keep him in politics. He wrote, "God Almighty has set before me two great objects, the suppression of the Slave Trade and the Reformation of Manners [morals]."[1] A decade later he reiterated the conviction about racial injustice: "The grand object of my parliamentary existence [is the abolition of the slave trade]. . . . Before this great cause all others dwindle in my eyes."[2]

Wilberforce would need this strong sense of divine call, for the battle for racial justice consumed almost forty-six years of his life (1787–1833). Eleven times the House of Commons defeated his motion to end the slave trade. Opponents threatened his life. Men who he thought were good friends severed ties with him. Political pressure to back down escalated, threatening his re-elections. If they abolished slavery, West Indian assemblies announced they would declare independence from Britain and federate with the United States.

One stimulant to Wilberforce's persistence came from pastor John Newton, himself a former slave trader. He reinforced Wilberforce's own belief that God wanted him to pursue this cause at all costs. He told Wilberforce, "It is hoped and believed that the Lord has raised you up for the good of His church and for the good of the nation."[3] Newton urged him to stay in public life as a context for carrying out his calling. Another contemporary, John Wesley, told him in a letter, "Unless God raised you up for this very thing, you will be worn out by the opposition of man and devils. But if God be for you, who can be against you?"[4]

His passionate speeches, rooted in biblical values, gradually eroded resistance. Twenty years after his first motion, a majority voted for abolition, resulting in a torrent of tears streaming down Wilberforce's face. Yet that vote ended the slave *trade*, not slavery itself. He fought twenty-six more years before Parliament voted in 1833 to outlaw slave ownership in all British colonies. The vote occurred three days after Wilberforce died.

No matter where or how you serve the Lord, steadfastness depends on knowing God put you there.

Dig Deeper

Read the story of Wilberforce's tireless effort for racial justice in John Piper's *The Roots of Endurance*. What stitches together the three historical figures featured in this book, including John Newton and Charles Simeon, are factors that instilled invincible perseverance.

Another meaningful book on tenacity in Christian living is Gordon MacDonald's *A Resilient Life* (Nelson, 2004). In a chapter titled "Resilient People Listen for a Call from God," he differentiates between a *call* to a particular responsibility or purpose and God's *leading* to a specific position. He identifies several "call stories" in Scripture and explains how people can discern the genuineness of a call from God.

CHAPTER 7

Rousing
the Enemy

As soon as the wheels of the jetliner skidded on
the runway in Cochin, India, it happened.

Totally unexpected.

Soul-jarring.

The eager anticipation for my teaching stint at Gospel for Asia
Seminary suddenly evaporated, leaving my spirit in a pall of darkness
that rivaled the low-lying thunderheads hovering over the airport.
Overwhelming despair enveloped me. Horrific fear and heart-acceler-
ating anxiety clamped down my attitude with a python-like grip. After
my pick up, and for over two hours on the road, I sat in a stupor, unable
to carry on a conversation. I regretted coming and mentally scrounged
for an excuse to tell the driver to turn around and go back to the airport
where I could catch the next flight home.

Arriving at my destination, I lay prostrate on the floor of my room
alternately crying, praying, and quoting Scripture from memory, desperate for relief from the unfathomable apprehension that left me gasping

for a deep breath. I phoned my wife—at 2 a.m. her time—sobbing and begging her for the okay to come home immediately.

The oppression gradually subsided, lasting only for a twenty-four-hour period. And over the next two weeks, I enjoyed stimulating interaction on church leadership with fifty responsive students, who, after graduation, would penetrate India and surrounding countries with the gospel.

I figured that what happened in India was a mystifying, once-in-a-lifetime occurrence. I didn't expect a repeat two years later as my plane approached Colombo, Sri Lanka.

I couldn't have been more wrong.

In Singapore, I had spent the two previous days sightseeing and catching up on sleep. I boarded the plane well-rested, optimistic, and grateful for the chance to see the world and serve the church at large. But the physical and emotional upheaval as I walked to baggage in Colombo mimicked Cochin: a smothering dread, a revulsion toward the people and sights around me, and an aching loneliness. Sri Lanka was the last place on earth I wanted to be. Once again, the terrorist attack on my psyche lasted for hours, eventually repelled by SOS prayers and recitation of every Bible promise I could retrieve.

Seasoned missionaries and biblical scholars I subsequently consulted explained the phenomenon: *a spiritual attack*. I had invaded enemy-held territory, countries dominated by the false religions of Hinduism and Buddhism. When someone goes to such a locale to train nationals to teach the Bible or to lead churches, Satan doesn't take it lightly.

Unlikely Source of Encouragement

I'm not someone who looks for a demon behind every bush, who sensationalizes every setback or affliction as a satanic attack. Yet the Bible makes it clear that Satan opposes Christ and his church.

My purpose in this chapter isn't to unpack the doctrine of Satan or to convey strategies for defeating him. Helpful tomes on these subjects dot the shelves of Christian bookstores.[1] My aim is fastened to the theme of encouragement that stitches together all the pages of this book. Here's the point of this chapter: *when you encounter Satan's opposition to what you're doing for Christ, it means you're a threat to him. Your service is important; otherwise, why would he try to impede it?!*

In *Thirsting for God*, Gary Thomas echoes my point:

> Surprisingly enough, Christian writers from centuries past found some measure of comfort in the difficulty of satanic opposition. Climacus, who warned of the reality of demonic opposition, also reminded us that being shot at is evidence that we are fighting. The Christian should not fear this difficulty—it is a sign of progress. Instead, we should fear the lack of opposition, for its absence means the enemy has found us unworthy of opposition.[2]

My New Testament professor, Merrill C. Tenney, once told his class, "The devil never opposes insignificant work." Yet he *will* try to unsettle a preacher before he enters the pulpit. He'll hinder the Wycliffe missionary who labors painstakingly to translate the Gospel of Mark into a tribal language. He'll distract the businessman over lunch right before he starts sharing the plan of salvation with an associate. And Satan will disrupt the Sunday school teacher on the way to church, where she intends to plant seeds of the gospel in the minds and hearts of elementary children.

Satan's modus operandi isn't usually a frontal assault, such as the spiritual panic attacks I experienced. Rather, when we commit to a new ministry or while we're engaged in it, he may ramp up temptations to sin in an area where we've long been vulnerable. A series of aggravating circumstances may converge, siphoning off time and energy from our service venture. Weaknesses of temperament may be magnified for a time, resulting in a fragility that almost incapacitates us; or self-recrimination escalates over past mistakes or concerning a grown child's not following the Lord, goading us to quit, trying to convince us we aren't qualified to serve. As Jerry Rankin puts it, "Spiritual warfare is not so much about demon possession, [or] territorial spirits . . . as it is overcoming Satan's lies and deceits in our own life."[3]

Anticipating spiritual warfare doesn't ease its intensity. But in the heat of battle, let's draw strength from the ironic perspective that Satan's adversarial reaction exposes the significance of our service.

Now let's identify biblical examples of Satan's penchant to oppose the Lord's servants.

Cause and Effect

His very name reveals his adversarial nature. "Satan" means "opponent," from a verb "to lie in wait." Peter compared him to a hungry lion who's stalking prey, seeking his next meal (1 Pet. 5:8). In Ephesians 6:12, Paul insisted, "Our struggle is not against flesh and blood, but against the rulers, against the powers, against the world forces of this darkness, against the spiritual *forces* of wickedness in the heavenly *places*." Three episodes in Acts demonstrate Satan's propensity to go on the offensive in response to persons making inroads for the gospel. These occurrences are representative of many more in the first-century church.

Scene 1: Acts 16:6–24

Early in Paul's second missionary trip, God revised his team's travel itinerary, redirecting them to Macedonia through a vision. In Philippi, the Lord opened Lydia's heart, creating receptivity to Paul's proclamation of the gospel. No sooner had she and her household been baptized than Satan fomented opposition.

A demon-possessed slave girl followed Paul around, pestering him to such an extent that he performed an exorcism. Her owners, deprived of the money she made through fortunetelling, dragged him and Silas before the authorities, accusing them of rebellion against Roman customs. The evangelists suffered severe beatings and confinement.

The timing wasn't coincidental. Satan-induced adversaries validated the strategic importance of the first converts in a new geographic region.

Scene 2: Acts 17:1–10

On the subsequent leg of their trip, starting in the synagogue at Thessalonica, Paul explained how Christ had fulfilled Old Testament prophecies of the Messiah. A few Jews believed, followed by a large number of Gentiles and leading women of the region. Paul's apologetic angered other Jews, who formed a mob and tried to sway civil authorities by claiming the visitors were "upsetting the world" (v. 4). The hostile threats prompted locals to whisk Paul and his companions away by night.

Yet another indication that when Christ is proclaimed, Satan doesn't sit still.

Scene 3: Acts 19

The news of a resurrected Christ also received an incendiary reaction among some folks in Ephesus. For two years, Paul used Ephesus as his base and "all who lived in Asia heard the word of the Lord, both Jew and Greeks" (v. 10). Through preaching and miraculous phenomena, "the name of the Lord Jesus was being magnified" (v. 17). Occult practitioners demonstrated their new allegiance to Christ by burning their books in a bonfire.

No wonder those who crafted idols for a living incited a riot against Paul, and organized a pep rally for the false goddess Artemis.

Stories of such spiritual struggles unfold throughout church history. The more the borders of Christianity expanded, the more battles intensified.

Wartime Mentality

When you intercede for a lost loved one or for a missionary who's on the front lines in a difficult Muslim country, Satan will taunt you with the long odds against a positive reply from God.

When you prepare for Sunday's message or for the Bible discussion with your small group, he'll discourage you with the absurdity of God using someone as sinful and as weak as you to tell others how to live.

When you accept the invitation to the office of elder or deacon, when you agree to mentor teens, to administer a Christian school, or to plan your church's missions festival, in some way, shape, or form, Satan's counterattack is inevitable.

Expect a long and drawn out fight. Christ's church is a battleship, not a cruise ship.

Wield every spiritual weapon at your disposal.

But don't get so discouraged or disillusioned that you throw down your weapons and go AWOL. When foes outnumber you, when victory seems elusive, when battle fatigue coaxes you to raise a white flag, remember that the firepower coming your way shows how integral you are to the war effort.

Dig Deeper

Take a couple devotional times to digest these Bible passages: Psalm 119:9–11; Proverbs 27:17; Matthew 4:1–11; 2 Corinthians 10:3–5; Ephesians 6:10–20; Galatians 6:2. Ponder these questions:

What strategies for fighting the enemy do these texts unveil?

Which of these weapons do you wield most often? Which means of victory are you currently neglecting?

Hone in on Matthew 4:1–11. What does this narrative tell us about Satan? How is it helpful to know each of these characteristics or strategies of our enemy?

At the tail end of Paul's treatise on spiritual warfare, he specifically solicited prayers for his own effectiveness in proclaiming the gospel (Eph. 6:18–20). Right now, think of a missionary or church staff member. Intercede for this person's ministry of teaching or evangelism. Then write a hand-written note informing him or her of your prayers, and drop it in the mail.

CHAPTER 8

THE BLESSING FACTOR

WHEN SOMEBODY LASHES OUT AT YOU, LACERATING YOUR HEART WITH VENOMOUS WORDS, WHERE DO YOU TURN? When you want to vent, yet you need the perspective of someone besides your precious spouse, but you can't trust just anybody to keep your confidence and you know a phone call won't suffice because you're too upset, whose doorbell do you ring?

I showed up at the doorstep of my new friend, David. We were full-time associate staff members of a large midwestern church. When his wife opened the door, I entreated through tears, "Esther, can I borrow David for a while?"

His sympathetic presence and prayers assuaged the sting from the painful encounter with someone in the church earlier that day. That happened thirty-five years ago. David's and Esther's ongoing friendship—cultivated by scores of meals, hundreds of genial conversations, repeated intercessions, and a few overnight trips together—is hands-down the most rewarding outcome of those years on the church staff. To this day, they are gap-fillers in my life.

Bountiful Blessings

The friendship with David and Esther represents one of the blessings God has bestowed on me through my decades of service to him: *the fellowship of co-laborers*. Whether you're a church volunteer or a vocational Christian worker, one way God gives back to you is the provision of companionship that often spills over from the work environment.

The enriching bond that develops among some folks who serve together is one aspect of a heartening perspective on ministry that Don Cousins calls "the blessing factor."[1] In a nutshell, *God intends to bless us through what we do for him.* Grasping this viewpoint increases incentive for the time, energy, and other forms of sacrifice integral to the tasks he assigns.

I'm aware that some people who serve, especially church volunteers, often feel used by the leaders who recruit them. They view themselves as slot-fillers who exist to fulfill somebody else's agenda. Once they assume a position, they're often taken for granted, receiving little in the way of recognition or training. But that isn't how God operates. Don Cousins elaborates:

> God is not a "user" of people. He cares about *you*, not what you can do for Him. He doesn't even need us to do anything for Him. He calls us to His work in order to give *us* something: He pours out His blessings, out of which we're able to bless others. . . . God is a giver, not a taker.[2]

The pages that follow reveal the types of blessing that stem from serving Christ.

Deeper Intimacy with God

Ministering to others doesn't merely introduce them to Christ or facilitate their spiritual growth. Serving them also bolsters *our* faith and enhances *our* walk with the Lord.

As a Bible teacher, do you recall the last time a Bible passage you studied and taught pricked your own conscience, spawning repentance? The time a lesson or sermon you delivered shed light on a pressing circumstance in *your* life, informing a decision? Do you remember when a divine promise that you conveyed to others injected hope within *you* for a brighter future? God blesses *you* through the Word you employ to bless others.

As a personal witness, how often has your burden for a lost friend, family member, or coworker driven you to your knees, where you pleaded for God to open their heart? As a pastor, when has a perplexing church matter or the threat of an unreasonable critic generated a desperate cry for the Lord's wisdom? When did you last whisper "thanks" to the Lord for giving you the right words to share with a hurting person or for the change of heart he cultivated in a separated couple who reconciled? How can prayer, regardless of the reason, *not* result in more intimate fellowship with the Lord?

Involvement in the Lord's work compels us to seek him, which is the main thing he wants from us: "The Lord has looked down from heaven upon the sons of men to see if there are any who understand, Who seek after God" (Ps. 14:2). If I'm concerned at all about effectiveness, complacency in my relationship with him isn't an option. Nothing deepens my knowledge of God like having to rely on him while striving to meet desperate human needs in a fallen world.

Serving fuels friendship with the Lord, which in turn empowers our ministry. It's a reciprocal relationship. There's no doubt in my mind that if I weren't heavily vested in his work, I'd enjoy less intimacy with Christ. Bob Cousins echoes this benefit of service: "God calls me to His work in order to strengthen our relationship."[3]

Maximum Meaning

I want to make it crystal clear that the primary source of our identity and significance as persons is Christ's work for us on the cross, *never* what we do for him. (See Chapter Twenty-Four, "Source of Your Significance.") But with that qualification out of the way, our investment in ministry is nonetheless a consequential source of purpose and identity—more than enough reason to get out of the bed in the morning.

In the fall of 2008, due to a mortgage debt crisis, investors in the United States stock market lost an average of 36 percent of their money. No one can guarantee the principal, much less the dividends, of what we put into the market. But whether you teach, witness, intercede, mentor, administer church programs—you name it!—investments in God's work enjoy *permanence*.

Go on a safari in Scripture for what lasts forever, and you'll find two things: the *souls of people* and *God's revelation*. In John 5:28–29, Jesus asserted that everybody in the tombs will one day come forth to a resurrection of either life or judgment. Hebrews 9:27 complements Jesus' words, announcing, "It is appointed for men to die once and after this comes judgment." Every person you meet or serve has an eternal destiny. Peter accentuated the perpetual nature of God's Word, piggybacking off a verse from Isaiah 40:

> You have been born again, not of seed which is perishable but imperishable, *that is*, through the living and abiding Word of God,
> For
>
> > "All flesh is like grass,
> > And all its glory like the flower of grass.
> > The grass withers,
> > And the flower falls off,
> >
> > but the word of the Lord abides forever." (1 Pet. 1:23–24)

So leading a ladies' Bible study group, teaching a Sunday school class, or recruiting those who do are rock-solid ways to invest.

Imagine this: no matter what spiritual gift you exercise or in what venue you serve, you are buying stock in at least one of those enduring entities—people and God's Word. The next time pressure, discouragement, or any form of spiritual warfare impinges on enjoyment of your ministry, remember this blessing: your life packs more meaning because what you do matters forever.

*For a more thorough treatment of guaranteed dividends in ministry, see Chapter Seventeen, "Reaping What You Sow."

Forever Friends

Previously I illustrated the blessing of friendships fueled by serving together. Rubbing elbows with others on the church staff, in Sunday school, or in the choir fosters fellowship because in those service venues, we spot traits that attract us. We're awed by an associate's creative thinking during brainstorming sessions. You notice the balance of firmness and sensitivity with which a teaching partner handles a first-grader's behavior problem. You observe how a team member "listens with her heart" during conversations. Prayers together about ministry concerns reveal like-mindedness. Before you know it, you're sharing meals in each other's homes or playing golf together.

While he awaited execution in a Roman cell, Paul put a premium on relationships cultivated as a church planter. In the fourth chapter of 2 Timothy, he pleaded for Timothy and John Mark to visit him. He favorably cited thirteen other individuals by name who had at some point served alongside him.

It isn't just what we do that blesses us, it's *who we get to do it with*. Outside your family members, who would you feel comfortable calling at 3 A.M.? More often than not, the names on this short list are persons with whom you've served the Lord in some capacity.

Multiplying Yourself

A fourth God-given blessing emanating from our ministry is watching God use persons we've recruited, motivated, and trained. It isn't just what we do that's satisfying, but what we enable others to do for him.

More gratifying than leading my own group Bible study is observing a student I've trained do it with excellence. More rewarding than publishing an article I've written is seeing the byline of someone I assisted in the polishing of her manuscript.

The director of children's ministry experiences this element of "the blessing factor" when she recruits and equips a reluctant couple to teach kids, then watches them thrive in that venue for over a decade. She can name kids who've come to faith in Christ through the couple who initially thought they weren't cut out to work with children. God also gives back in this fashion to the person who shows a new believer how to share his faith, then finds out that his protégé led six persons to Christ within a year.

Multiplying yourself through others necessarily involves the discovery and exercise of their spiritual gifts. How has God's Spirit enabled them and put them together to serve in the church, community, or world for his glory? When you find folks who are serious about ministry involvement, go over the following questions with them. If you mobilize them to serve Christ, you're also setting them up to experience "the blessing factor."

- What do I enjoy doing for the Lord or for other people? What brings me the most satisfaction? Is there any realm of service that makes me think, *I was made for this!*
- Which of my ministry efforts has God apparently blessed in the past? In the realm of service, when have I most sensed his presence and his power?

- How have others encouraged or complimented me in relation to ministry? What efforts have older, more mature Christians affirmed?
- In what ministry venues am I most comfortable? Do I flourish more in behind-the-scenes, less formal settings, or am I at home up front, leading a committee or group?
- What has God's Spirit communicated to me about ministry by means of inner promptings? Is there something I feel compelled to do or to try?
- A person's gifts or competencies often emerge as a result of activity or engagement. What needs in the church or community can I volunteer to help meet?
- What ministry burden or passion has God given me? What piece of God's heart for the church, community, or world do I carry?

The high costs of serving the Lord are undeniable. But the blessings we receive are equally indisputable.

Dig Deeper

How do the Bible verses that follow correlate with the blessings of service cited in this chapter?

Psalm 16:11
John 15:16
Proverbs 17:17
2 Timothy 2:2

Part Two

When You Feel Inadequate

Weakness, fragility, and lack of confidence plague many persons in God's labor force. Chapters in this section help us shift the spotlight off ourselves and onto God. How refreshing to discover that God uses unlikely folks to accomplish extraordinary things so *he*, rather than we, receives the acclaim.

CHAPTER 9

CAPTAIN OF
THE *ARE NOTS*

THERE WAS A BAFFLING CHASM BETWEEN WHO HE *WAS*
AND WHAT HE *DID*, BETWEEN HIS CREDENTIALS AND HIS
accomplishments.

Raised in a poor family, the boy's formal education was spotty, lasting only several years. Even as an adult, misspellings pockmarked his
letters. A reporter who heard him speak to a large audience in England
lamented the preacher's incapacity to grasp basic grammar, saying, "He
butchered the King's English!"

When he moved to Boston at seventeen to work in his uncle's shoe
store, a prerequisite for the job was church attendance. Edward Kimball,
who taught the young men's Sunday school class, said he had met "few
persons whose minds were spiritually darker."[1] Kimball led the young
man to Christ, but church leaders rejected his initial application for
membership. Kimball admitted, "The committee of the Mount Vernon
Church seldom met an applicant for membership more unlikely ever to
become a Christian of clear and decided views of the Gospel truth, still
less to fill any extended sphere of public usefulness."[2]

But God has a sense of humor. He enjoys confounding man's opinion and circumventing human wisdom. Dwight L. Moody (1837–1899), a trophy of God's grace, catapulted to international renown as an evangelist, becoming a household name among believers in the United States and Great Britain. Crowds of up to twenty thousand attended his meetings. One audience included the United States president and his cabinet. The education-deprived evangelist started a Bible school that thrives today as Moody Bible Institute in Chicago.

The same British reporter who criticized Moody's poor grammar was bewildered by his effectiveness with an audience. Citing the emotional reaction of listeners and their responsiveness to Moody's invitation to accept Christ, he exclaimed that he couldn't find a natural reason for Moody's success.

Moody agreed with the assessment, admitting that there was no *natural* reason for his attainments! One of his early biographers concluded, "Here in the life of Moody is a divine apologetic, putting hope into our one-talent lives by proving endowment and advantage to be, in God's sight, small as the dust of the balance; that my uttermost for His highest must never be an inventory of genius, but a program of consecration."[3] The same author insisted, "Our beleaguered age stands in need, not so much of ten-talent men as God-conquered commoners."[4]

Moody's own life proved to be "Exhibit A" of the most famous quote attributed to him: "The world has yet to see what God will do with and for and through and in and by the man who is fully and wholly consecrated to Him."[5]

But Moody was far more than an evangelist, preacher, and Bible school founder. Here's the tag that best fits him: he was the preeminent *are not.*

Allow me to explain by delving into a reassuring text in 1 Corinthians.

Unlikely Choices

Two factors molded the thinking of inhabitants in the ancient city of

Corinth: the Roman Empire's elevation of social status and Greek culture's emphasis on human learning and eloquence. In chapter one of 1 Corinthians, Paul took pains to explain the disparity between God's criteria for choosing people and society's basis for acceptance, between God's wisdom and human cleverness.

Paul admitted that the message of the cross appears foolish to some, yet called it "the power of God" to persons believing in Christ (1 Cor. 1:18). Then he concluded, "The foolishness of God is wiser than men" (1 Cor. 1:25). To illustrate the radical difference between how God thinks and operates compared to the world, Paul cited the makeup of the church he had previously planted in Corinth. The term "calling" in the ensuing text refers to God's initiative in their salvation:

> For consider your calling, brethren, that there were not many wise according to the flesh, not many mighty, not many noble; but God has chosen the foolish things of the world to shame the wise, and God has chosen the weak things of the world to shame the things which are strong, and the base things of the world and the despised God has chosen, the things that are not, so that He may nullify the things that are, so that no man may boast before God. (1 Cor. 1:26–29)

To launch a Christian presence in the city, God didn't cherry pick from among the area's elite citizenry. He didn't prioritize the well-educated (*not many wise*). He didn't select folks who wielded political clout (*not many mighty*). The Lord didn't choose wealthy aristocrats who would guarantee the congregation's financial security and cement its social standing (*not many noble*).

No, God turned things topsy-turvy, opting for persons perceived as *foolish*, *weak*, *base*, and *despised*. Then Paul put an exclamation mark on God's perplexing selections by saying he had chosen "the things that *are not*" (emphasis mine).

The "are not" phrase refers to things that, for all practical purposes, don't exist. Here, it's an allusion to people who simply don't count, who are of little consequence in the eyes of those who exert authority or boast worldly status.[6]

Why does God then use in ministry such unlikely candidates? "That no man should boast before God," Paul asserted. The achievements of servants who aren't expected to succeed put the spotlight on God's gracious enablement. Others look at such a person's life and ministry, concluding, "The only explanation for his (or her) success is that *God did it!*"

*See Chapter Ten, "How God Gets Glory," for more on God's habit of using improbable people.

The Holy Spirit's Interrogation

Allow God's Spirit to question you in relation to 1 Corinthians 1:26–29. Think of the various venues in which you've served the Lord, the different roles you've assumed, then hone in on your current responsibilities.

Do you recall a time you acted unwisely, perhaps even foolishly? Do you ever get frustrated because you lack the authority or status to make important things happen? Do you ever feel that you don't qualify for usefulness due to inherent weaknesses of your flesh or temperament? Do you ever view yourself as despicable or ignoble? Has anyone ever belittled or despised you for your witness, or for tough decisions you've made as a leader? Do others ever disrespect or consider inconsequential who you are or what you do for the Lord?

Do you ever feel like an *are not*?

If you answer affirmatively to any of those questions, you're a top contender for an extravagantly fruitful ministry. Why? When results occur, you're less likely to boast and more apt to reflect the grace and sufficiency of Christ.

Like Dwight L. Moody.

I'll close with yet another story of how God uses unlikely people so *he*, rather than *they*, receives the credit.

Testimony of God's Grace

This is the story of a flawed but faithful servant of God whom I know. By all accounts, he has served effectively on two large church staffs. For over thirty years, he has utilized his PhD to teach at a prestigious Christian university. To supplement his ministry on the faculty, he goes overseas to train national church leaders. Though far from a well-known figure, he has written or co-authored eighteen books and over a hundred articles.

But to hear him tell it, any fruitfulness in his life borders on the miraculous.

As an eleven-year-old, his view of sexuality was skewed, yet his curiosity piqued by watching his mom have sex in a motel room with a man he didn't know. She took him along during an out-of-state motel fling with a co-worker, then abandoned him, phoning his dad to cross the state line to pick him up—*after* she and the stranger had driven away.

Painfully shy and hampered by low self-image, he didn't date in high school, figuring any girl he asked out would turn him down. During chaperoned dances in the school gym after Friday night games, he sat alone in a dark corner of the bleachers, weeping and loathing himself because he wasn't *normal*.

A month after graduating from high school, he literally beat himself up, pummeling his head time and again with his own balled-up fists, cursing himself for low grades and social clumsiness. He had daydreamed and written poetry during classes, resulting in a low C average and an SAT score so low that the university he wanted to attend rejected his application.

After finishing college elsewhere, he remembers the embarrassment of an anemic performance on a Miller Analogies test required by a graduate school. Seventy-two percent of test-takers earned a higher score.

During adult years, depression has dogged his steps. The pendulum of emotion swings from a numb, robotic, can't-feel-a-thing state all the way across the spectrum to a hypersensitivity marked by heartache and uncontrollable bouts of weeping.

To this day, he'd be the first to admit that he's fragile and struggles with sin to an extent he considers inconsistent with Christian maturity. He enjoys an outrageously happy marriage, yet the insecurity that plagued his adolescence still impinges on other relationships. Having an emotional tank with a larger-than-normal capacity to fill, he sometimes expects too much from those brave souls who love him. He's prone to magnify slights and projects his own sense of inferiority onto others' view of him. Even one of the couple's closest friends confided to his wife with exasperation, "He's too needy for us."

Yet propelled by a strong sense of call to communicate God's Word and to train others for ministry, he keeps putting one foot in front of the other each day. What sustains this man is his deep conviction that God's promises are more reliable than his own fickle feelings. And when he's despondent, though he fights for his joy, he reminds himself not to expect on earth what God only promised for heaven.

No wonder this person considers 1 Corinthians 1:26–29 among his favorite Bible passages! These verses imbue hope that God will use him in spite of a history of instability. After teaching on this text in a church he received a call the next day from someone who had heard him. The caller asked to speak to the "Captain of the *Are Nots*"!

I was the person who answered the phone that day. Dwight L. Moody isn't the only servant of Christ whose usefulness exceeded expectations. *It's my story, too.*

The jury is in, and the verdict is: persons who apparently don't qualify for fruitful ministry are the ones who, in the reverse logic of God, are the prime candidates to reap eternal dividends.

Soli Deo gloria! Glory to God!

Dig Deeper

Throughout *Serve Strong*, I intersperse stories about Christian leaders of bygone eras. Reading biographies of men and women God greatly used is like a fresh intake of oxygen for my suffocating soul. I can't urge you strongly enough to read about Augustine, Jonathan Edwards, David Brainerd, John Newton, George Whitefield, John Wesley, William Wilberforce, John Bunyan, Hudson Taylor, Amy Carmichael, Robert Murray McCheyne, Dwight L. Moody, and others.

Pastor and author John Piper testifies, "Good biographies of great Christians make for remarkably efficient reading. . . . Biographies have served as much as any other human source in my life to overcome the inertia of mediocrity. . . . [They] charge my pastoral batteries and give me guidance and encouragement."[7]

As you read a biography, ponder these questions:

What made this person's story worth publishing?
What personal qualities help explain his or her effectiveness?
What evidences of God's grace and enablement do you find?
What part of the book most challenged you? Why?
What part of the story encouraged you most? Why?

CHAPTER 10

How God Gets Glory

What engenders a desperate state of mind within you? What weakness or threatening situation leaves you feeling utterly helpless or needy? What prompts an attitude of absolute dependence on God's intervention?

What constitutes a deep-felt need or sense of helplessness differs among God's servants. Perhaps it's the unrealistic deadline or workload your supervisor gave. The church critic who isn't mature enough to meet with you face-to-face and resorts to backstabbing in conversations with other members. An estranged daughter who once again rebuffs your attempt to reconcile.

Or what requires God's intervention may be weaknesses of temperament that have come to a head, leaving you with little fuel to run on. Or the inability to make financial ends meet due to a recent proliferation of medical bills. Perhaps it's a drought of observable results in your sphere of service or an ever-widening time gap between vocational ministry positions.

For me, it's another tense encounter with my younger grown son who has Asperger Syndrome. One verbal sparring match occurred the same week I taught leaders on the subject of conflict management, instilling doubts about my qualifications, causing me to feel hopeless concerning our relationship. Other times it's another bout of joy-sapping depression, blanketing me, smothering initiative, making routine responsibilities more challenging.

I'm learning, ever-so-slowly, to view afflictions of this sort as opportunities to display God's glory through my life and ministry. Before I elaborate on this perspective, allow me to dissect the concept of God's glory. Grasping it is essential for absorbing the principle framing this chapter.

God Is Heavy

The Bible's emphasis on God's *glory* refers to his *weight*. That's the root concept of the noun "glory" and the verb "glorify." God is heavy in the figurative sense of significance or importance. God insists that he created us for his glory (Isa. 43:7). The psalmist cried, "Not to us, O Lord, not to us, But to Your name give glory" (Ps. 115:1). Paul wrote, "Whatever you do, do all to the glory of God" (1 Cor. 10:31). John Piper goes so far as to say, "God's aim in creating the world was to display the value of his own glory."[1]

Closely connected to the concept of God's glory is the notion of honoring God, which carries the idea of *worthiness* or *deserving a return*. Your church gives an *honorarium* to a guest preacher or conference leader, suggesting that he or she deserves a monetary investment. First Timothy 6:16 represents many other verses when it salutes the superlative value of Christ: "To Him *be honor* and eternal dominion" (emphasis on "honor" mine).

Here are the questions on which this chapter hinges: *How do we best glorify God? How can we most effectively magnify his significance and demonstrate his worth?*

Now let's explore the relationship between God's glory and our desperate needs.

Weakness Is the Way

When he pays the price of mundane, unglamorous, yet vital hours of preparation, does the Bible teacher glorify God? Yes.

Does the missionary couple's choice to leave behind family and friends to go overseas honor him? Of course.

Does the homemaker's winsome presentation of the gospel to a neighbor over coffee convey God's worth? Undoubtedly.

When we repel a nagging temptation—*again*—or exhibit uncompromising character under pressure, do we make him look good? Absolutely.

Yet I'm convinced that it's our weakness, not strength; our neediness, not sterling psychological health; our brokenness, not stability; our inadequacy, not unflagging confidence; and our dire circumstances, not trouble-free days, which offer the greater opportunity to enhance God's reputation among the persons we meet, know, and serve. A reassuring irony of Christian living is that he receives more glory through our fragility and in threatening situations, because that's when we most need him. *That's when God gets the chance to throw his weight around.*

The deep roots of this claim grow in the fertile soil of Psalm 50:15. The Lord invites us, "Call upon Me in the day of trouble; I shall rescue you, and you will honor Me."

When we feel weak or inadequate, we're forced to trust him since there's no other recourse. We're prompted to pray due to the limits of our resourcefulness and the press of outside forces. Then God answers our plea and displays his power in some manner. He fortifies us or alters circumstances and we praise him as a result. We tell others what God did. Being at wit's end magnifies his name because he gets a chance to do what only he can do.

I'm indebted to John Piper, whose comments on Psalm 50:15 acquainted me with this truth. His take on this pivotal verse motivates me to call on God when I'm afflicted so he'll get to display his might and receive applause. Piper insists that we glorify God "not by serving Him, but being served by Him. . . [We] do not glorify God by providing His needs, but by praying that He would provide ours—and trusting Him to answer."[2] According to Piper, "The Giver gets the glory. We get help."[3]

A towering figure from the past illustrates this principle.

Grace and Glory

More than a century before satellites beamed Christian TV programs across the globe, Charles Spurgeon (1834–1892) was a renowned British pastor. Due to the depth and eloquence of his preaching, contemporaries considered him the greatest biblical expositor of his era. He spoke to jam-packed sanctuaries while still in his twenties. So many folks in London wanted to hear him preach that he occasionally pleaded with church members to stay home so unsaved visitors could get a seat and hear the gospel. Spurgeon's mental gifts dwarfed typical Christian leaders. Publishers still disseminate his devotional books and sermons throughout the world.

At first glance, you'd think he's the last person to feel inadequate or dependent. Surely the strengths of this behemoth of Church history far eclipsed his weaknesses.

Wrong.

Recurring depression dogged Spurgeon most of his adult life. His first episode descended at age twenty-four. Here's what he wrote about it: "My spirits were sunken so low that I could weep by the hour like a child, and yet I knew not what I wept for."[4] Repeated incidences spawned these words: "Causeless depression cannot be reasoned with. . . . As well fight with the mist as with this shapeless, indefinable, yet all-beclouding hopelessness."[5] In a sermon titled "When a Preacher Is Downcast," he modeled transparency long before it was in vogue: "The strong are not always vigorous, the wise not always ready, the brave not always courageous, and the joyous not always happy. . . . Good men are promised tribulation in this world, and ministers may expect a larger share than others, that they may learn sympathy with the Lord's suffering people, and so may be fitting shepherds of an ailing flock."[6]

Painful gout attacks impaired him physically, especially as he aged. In 1888, as he lay prostrate with this debilitating form of arthritis, he said, "I cannot get better till I am in another climate, and I cannot reach that other climate till I get better."[7] He's the commentator whose take on Psalm 50:15 informed John Piper. Of that verse Spurgeon said, "Here is a . . . covenant that God enters into with you who pray to Him, and whom He helps. He says, 'You shall have the deliverance, but I must have the glory. . . . ' Here is a delightful partnership: we obtain that which we so greatly need, and all that God getteth is the glory which is due unto his name."[8]

Spurgeon understood experientially how human need magnifies the sufficiency of God. He wrote, "We shall bring our Lord most glory if we get from Him much grace."[9]

Psalm of My Life

During a lengthy, oppressive bout with depression, I wrote the following poem. It's an attempt to capture the faith-boosting perspective of Psalm 50:15 explored in this chapter.

HOW?

How can God receive most glory
in the plot of my life's story?
When I teach a class with flair,
or stop to show someone I care?
When I apply truth that I've heard,
or work to memorize his Word?

When I explain why I believe
to people willing to receive?
When I give away my stuff
to folks who do not have enough?
When I gladly pay the price
for some need-meeting sacrifice?
When others read the words I write
and benefit from my insight?
When my faith gets off the fence
and I start my day with confidence?

Or is the Lord more magnified
when my feeble hands are tied?
When I am mired knee-deep in need,
and I've no recourse but to plead
for Him to do what I cannot:
revive me, and improve my lot.

When I'm trapped at my wits' end,
and I've no choice but to depend
on wisdom I do not possess
to overcome the cause of stress?

Or when the devil turns up heat
and I am one step from defeat,
pleading for strength to resist
until he opens his closed fist?

Or when despondency descends;
I stumble in the fog it sends,
and the light can't penetrate,
and I groan under the weight

of a spirit without hope . . .
When I need Christ just to cope?

Or when I'm flat upon my face,
relying on sustaining grace,
weaned from pointless human pride . . .
is that when God's most glorified?
When only what the Lord can do
erases fear and sees me through?

Yes, his power gives me a song,
for when I'm weak, then he is strong.
Yes, his name is lifted up
when I extend an empty cup.

Dig Deeper

Think of a fruitful Christian worker you've known who has a faithful ministry despite physical frailty, painful circumstances, or weaknesses of temperament. Mull over these questions in relation to that person:

What factors in this person's life create extraordinary dependence on God?

What evidences of fruitfulness can you identify from his or her life or ministry?

How are God's power, sufficiency, and grace mirrored by this person?

How does this person's life and ministry cultivate hope within *you*?

CHAPTER 11

HARNESSING OUR POTENTIAL

The Blessing of Brokenness, Part 1

I WATCHED A TV WESTERN IN WHICH A COWBOY TRIED TO RIDE A WILD STALLION. FENCED IN BY A CORRAL, THE untamed horse—muscles rippling, snorting defiance—had never been ridden and had no intention of cooperating. Time and again, the ranch hand jumped on the brute's back only to be bucked. The cowboy's repeated efforts finally overcame the stallion's resistance. The horse succumbed to a saddle and rider and a bond developed between the two former foes.

Ranchers call this process "breaking a horse." Only by taming it, reducing it to submission, can they harness a wild stallion's potential.

Similarly, an unbridled soul restricts God's work in and through a person's life. In *Embracing Brokenness*, Alan Nelson concludes, "I doubt that people who have ever achieved significance, . . . or who have been used productively by the Holy Spirit in ministry, have eluded this process."[1]

Bettered by Brokenness

Most folks perceive a broken person as weak or emotionally fragile. When it comes to faith, they view brokenness as the polar opposite of a virile, trusting, stable Christian. But God's viewpoint differs. David wrote, "You do not delight in sacrifice, otherwise I would give it; You are not pleased with burnt offering. The sacrifices of God are a broken spirit; A broken and contrite heart, O God, You will not despise" (Ps. 51:16–17). What concerns God isn't so much what we do for him or religious acts of devotion as it is a poverty of spirit that stops bucking him at every turn.

Admittedly, a tragic event such as divorce or the sudden loss of a family member may devastate a person to such an extent that she can't cope with routine responsibilities. She needs time to heal, as well as friends or a counselor to help put her back together. But I'm not talking about a temporary state of brokenness as much as I am a settled, more permanent posture of one's heart, marked by tenderness and dependency.

A single event may produce an ongoing state of brokenness, but typical factors that create it include conviction and consequences of sin (as with King David), chronic physical infirmity, temperamental weaknesses, failure, or a long-lasting disappointment such as estrangement from a grown child or a career that never panned out. These factors may make us bitter or better. But when they wean us from self-reliance, instilling a yieldedness to Christ's control and a desperation for his enablement, it's a God-sanctioned mindset.

Despite the positive slant God puts on brokenness, Satan counters with lies that discourage us from ministry engagement. He tries to convince us that the past failure or the emotional fragility that may come with a broken spirit disqualifies us from fruitful service. Yet the very factor that we think hinders our impact may be the pivot on which an influential ministry turns.

Why is brokenness a prerequisite for rather than a hindrance to effective service? How does a God-pleasing state of brokenness show? This chapter and the next address those questions.

A Heart That's Humble

Unless the soul has been tamed, exceptional gifts or impressive accomplishment tend to breed arrogance.

For years, King Uzziah sought the Lord. God gave him material and military success. His fame spread. Yet the following commentary exposes the tendency of God's leaders to read their own press clippings: "He was marvelously helped until he was strong. But when he became strong, his heart was so proud that he acted corruptly, and he was unfaithful to the Lord his God" (2 Chron. 26:15–16).

A servant who is convinced of his potential for sin, who is scarred by painful experiences, whose flawed temperament puts a governor on selfish ambition, whose past failures or disappointments instill daily dependence on God's grace, is the kind of person who is less likely to boast, who defers to God's glory rather than his own. In a passage where God insists that only *he* has the right to rule, he said, "To this one I will look, To him who is humble and contrite of spirit, and who trembles at My word" (Isa. 66:2).

What kept Paul from self-exaltation, from boasting about a privileged experience of being "caught up in Paradise," was a *thorn in the flesh.* He viewed the thorn as an impediment to fruitfulness, pleading on three separate occasions for the Lord to remove it. God's response belongs in the memory banks of all wounded persons: "My grace is sufficient for you, for power is perfected in weakness" (2 Cor. 12:9). What Paul concluded about this restriction reveals an irony about brokenness: "Therefore I am well content with weaknesses, with insults, with distresses, with persecutions, with difficulties, for Christ's sake; for *when I am weak, then I am strong*" (2 Cor. 12:10, emphasis mine).

Keen awareness of our limitations compels us to rely on Christ's power. Well-intentioned servants often mimic the cry of Isaiah: "Here am I, send me!" (Isa. 6:8). But after a vision of the Lord and his holiness, *prior* to declaring his availability, Isaiah cried, "Woe is me, for I am ruined! Because I am a man of unclean lips" (Isa. 6:5).

Vance Havner lamented, "We are trying to get young people to volunteer and say, 'Here am I,' before they have ever said, 'Woe is me!'"[2] How else does brokenness show?

An Approach That's Authentic

A servant whose pride has been subdued is refreshingly authentic. Since what others think has waned in importance, she doesn't strive to project an image of invincibility or independence. She's transparent because you can see inside or through her. It's my contention that a worker who is transparent multiplies her impact for the Lord.

A transparent person isn't pretentious. She's considered "real" because she doesn't mask what's going on inside. She doesn't disclose every sin or secret indiscriminately, yet her prayer requests are specific and honest. She knows that others can't help bear her burdens unless she reveals those felt needs.

She's quick to seek support and counsel. She readily confesses sin to God and apologizes to others when it's called for. With discretion, she shares stories from her pilgrimage as a Christian in an effort to assist others. In conversations, counseling sessions, and teaching venues, she explains how a Bible text or truth has sustained or challenged her.

What convinces me of the positive effects of transparency are comments I've heard from Christian college students. In my doctoral dissertation research, I interviewed thirty students from two colleges. I asked for descriptions of faculty members who they held in high regard and whose behavior improved student-faculty relationships. Twenty-six out of thirty cited transparency as a positive trait that led to interaction. I heard these kinds of comments often about behavior that attracted them:

"When a teacher shows the down side of himself."
"When they share personal experiences."
"When an instructor talks about his own problems in daily living for God."

One student echoed the sentiment of others when he said, "It shows that a teacher understands what I'm going through." Another respondent remembered his youth ministry professor's testimony about a time she was "disappointed with God" and didn't feel connected to him. "I was having trouble with the same thing," he repeated, "and I could relate to her and we talked about it."

I'm not just coaxing you to be more transparent. My aim is to boost your spirits if you are a broken person, to convince you that woundedness fuels fruitfulness because the transparency it generates resonates with the people you are trying to serve.

*For a complementary perspective on the effects of transparency, see Chapter Fourteen, "The Power of Owning Up."

Your authenticity creates identification with you and instills hope in others who struggle or hurt. They start believing that the same Lord who sustains and uses you will do the same in and through them. Here's the spin put on this process by Ray Stedman: "Our earthiness must be as apparent to others as the power is so they may see that the secret is not us but God. That is why we must be transparent people, not hiding our weaknesses and failures, but honestly admitting them when they occur."[3]

It's okay that others see us as needy, so long as they see the sufficiency of Christ that keeps us going. That's how brokenness and subsequent transparency glorifies God.

Augustine, a fourth-century bishop and theologian whose writings left an indelible imprint on Christianity, demonstrated the impact of authenticity. His natural gifts and zeal for God resulted in a meteoric rise up the ecclesiastical ladder. Unflattering details of his pre-conversion years—rebellion, idleness, sexual immorality, thirst for fame—were quickly eclipsed by a burgeoning influence for God.

But he grew increasingly concerned about the gulf between his reputation as a church leader and his debauchery as a young man.

According to Gary Thomas, "The human side could have been lost, but Augustine decided to write his confessions and tell the whole story. . . . *The Confessions of Saint Augustine* remains one of the most widely read Christian books of all time."[4] Thomas added: "Augustine wanted people to see God's greatness, and he realized this is often best revealed through human weakness. To suppress his whole story would have been to rob God of the glory due Him for the remarkable work of transformation He accomplished in Augustine's life."[5]

To summarize, how does brokenness help harness our potential? A tamed soul keeps pride at bay and produces a healthy indifference to one's image, resulting in transparency. Far from restricting your usefulness to God, your wounds may expand it. The next chapter further illustrates this irony, and divulges two additional benefits of brokenness.

Dig Deeper

Procure a copy of Alan Nelson's *Embracing Brokenness* (NavPress, 2002). Nelson delves into far more detail on this theme than my two chapters in *Serve Strong*. Read this book for answers to these questions:

What is brokenness?

What is the difference between voluntary and involuntary brokenness?

What is the difference between being broken in the "wrong places" versus being broken in the "right places"?

What attitudes and behaviors indicate that a positive form of brokenness has occurred?

What is the correlation between brokenness and maturity?

CHAPTER 12

WANTED: WOUNDED SOLDIERS

The Blessing of Brokenness, Part 2

FOR YEARS, I BEGGED THE LORD TO HEAL ME OF CHRONIC DEPRESSION. THE INITIAL BENEFIT OF ANTI-DEPRESSANTS had waned. Though it is an avenue of divine grace for many persons, counseling hadn't alleviated my burden. And God's response to my pleading was silence.

I recall the day in 2003 when my perspective shifted. I concluded that the sovereignty of God is either a sterile doctrine or a dynamic reality. Could I trust him with my propensity for despondency? What were the implications of the fact that he had not heeded my cries for direct intervention? Was this my "thorn in the flesh" to keep me humble and dependent?

That's when the slant of my prayers also changed. Through tears, I surrendered my desire to be more emotionally whole. Here are the words I prayed:

Father, if You choose not to lift this veil of darkness, I accept that. I'm Yours. You're still good. You know what You're about. If this vulnerability to despondency always characterizes me, I'll assume You have a reason. I'll trust You to sustain me through the pain and use me in spite of it. What matters isn't that others perceive me as weak, but that they perceive You as strong.[1]

I didn't pray that glibly. I relented only after years of bucking the way God had put me together.

The previous chapter defined brokenness as a tamed soul that no longer bristles when God's will is difficult. I explained that a God-pleasing form of brokenness results in humility and transparency. Now I shift to two additional advantages of brokenness and to another illustration of this irony: *woundedness enhances rather than hinders usefulness to God.*

As my reference to depression indicated, I learned one benefit of brokenness the hard way.

A Spirit of Surrender

Going hand-in-glove with humility and transparency is a spirit of submission. Disappointment or other types of pain wean us from the felt need to have our way. A broken person realizes he is God's property and that God can do whatever he pleases with what is his. He takes Paul's words to the Corinthians to heart: "Do you not know that . . . you are not your own?" (1 Cor. 6:19). When it came to my own hypersensitivity and emotional makeup, I couldn't say, "No, Lord," and mean both words.[2]

When he followed God's directive to marry a harlot, then subsequently bought her again from a life of adultery, Hosea demonstrated a surrendered spirit (Hos. 1:2, 3:1). So did Isaiah when he obeyed the strange command to go naked and barefoot for three years as an object lesson against Egypt and Cush (Isa. 20:2–4). Ezekiel also exhibited this telltale mark of brokenness. There's no indication that Ezekiel balked when God sent him to warn the rebellious Israelites, even though he heard God say in the same breath that no one would listen to him (Ezek. 2–3).

When the Lord calls us to serve a difficult constituency, to move to a smaller congregation with less pay, or to invest time in a dysfunctional couple when we'd rather relax, we follow in the footsteps of the Old Testament prophets whose choices weren't governed by desire for personal gain, recognition, or comfort.

Whether we're resisting our temperamental makeup, rebelling against God's call to an unresponsive group, agitated over mistreatment, frustrated over gifts God never gave us, or bitter about doors that never opened, opposing the Lord impedes our usefulness. Surrender gives him the green light to deploy us however and whenever he pleases.

Now let's shift the spotlight to one more benefit of brokenness.

Service That's Selfless

My grandpa owned a mule. Every spring, instead of tossing out the mule's manure, he let it dry, then spread it over his freshly-planted corn, cucumbers, and okra. The manure fertilized the soil, preparing it for greater productivity.

That's a metaphor for the effect of brokenness on one's life and ministry. Though unappealing, it fertilizes the soul and enhances fruitfulness. What spurs our service is a selfless attitude, not a desire to inflate our self-esteem or improve our name recognition through accomplishment. We worry less about what folks think of us (because they seldom do anyway!). We stop using others' feedback to verify our self-worth.

I'm aware that sin still indwells a broken person. No one's incentive for ministry is entirely selfless. Yet whatever tames us puts a rein on impure motives and keeps them from stampeding out of control.

An honored alumnus of Columbia International University who endured numerous trials during decades of fruitful ministry on the mission field often prayed: "Lord Jesus, do absolutely anything you need to do *to* me, so that you can do absolutely everything you want to do *through* me."[3]

That's the utterance of a bridled soul. I'll close this chapter with the story of another broken, yet outrageously fruitful servant of God.

Productivity through Pain

For over thirty years, James "Buck" Hatch served on the faculty of Columbia Bible College in South Carolina, teaching courses in Bible, hermeneutics, psychology, and family life.[4] Hundreds, perhaps thousands, of alumni of what is now Columbia International University consider him their favorite and most influential professor. When he taught, students listened, riveted. When he counseled, hurting people received a life-sustaining injection of hope.

You'd think a dynamic personality and get-it-together psyche propelled such an enduring, respected ministry.

That wasn't the case.

His son Nathan called Buck Hatch "a painfully shy person, always near the brink of depression. . . . A soul not at home with itself."[5] Nathan's written tribute on his dad's eightieth birthday added, "My father has come to radiate a deep and abiding joy. But you could not call him a happy person. He has always wrestled with thorns in the flesh that drove him not to rely on himself."

Rather than yield to despair or conclude he wasn't fit for a vocational ministry, Buck gravitated to wounded people who judged themselves too severely and perceived God as aloof and uncaring. Ten hours a week he reserved for counseling, convincing hurting individuals that God is far more faithful and forgiving than folks imagine.

Prolific author Philip Yancey, a CIU alumnus, says that Buck's influence helped unpollute his faulty concepts of God. One student represented the views of many when he wrote to Buck, "You've been a father to hundreds of people who needed a father like you."

In my own forty-five years of vocational Christian service, I've never known a name spoken with more reverence than *Buck Hatch*. What a productive ministry from someone who was "insecure, melancholy, and introverted."

Nathan concluded that his dad's brokenness gave him ready access into the interior rooms of people's lives. "Buck Hatch's life demonstrated that the divine economy inverts natural priorities. In Christ's kingdom, the last shall be first, a life is saved by losing it, and weakness confounds strength." Having known Buck personally, I better understand a comment I heard from the late Joe Aldrich: "Only wounded soldiers can serve in God's army."[6]

It took a broken man to reach broken persons. In a world polluted by sin, deceived by Satan, and marred by dysfunctional relationships, who isn't in need of some repair? Rather than resist the process of brokenness, let it fertilize your soul and ministry.

Dig Deeper

In *Brokenness, Surrender, Holiness* (Moody Press, 2008), Nancy Leigh DeMoss discusses the necessity of brokenness over sin for personal and corporate revival. She defines brokenness, offers biblical examples, contrasts pride and brokenness, explains how to cooperate with God's Spirit in the process, plus offers her personal testimony.

Take her book with you the next time you go on a personal spiritual retreat. As you read, ask the Lord to expose the state and needs of your heart. This sentence from the book captures her slant: "You and I will never know God in revival until we first meet Him in brokenness" (42).

CHAPTER 13

FAILURE IS NOT FINAL

BRAD AND HIS WIFE, SUSAN, AREN'T SURE THEY'LL GO BACK TO THE FIELD AFTER THEIR FURLOUGH. TENSION with team members in the church-planting venture, combined with unresponsiveness of the nationals they tried to reach with the gospel, fosters discouragement and leaves them wondering if they correctly interpreted God's call.

Sally figured she'd thrive teaching first-graders. But six weeks after accepting the volunteer position, she dreads getting up on Sunday morning. She got off on the wrong foot the first day when six-year-old Timmy defiantly exclaimed, "I won't listen to a thing you say!"

Though he's known for incisive, passionate sermons and competent leadership of the church, Warren often feels deflated. His twenty-three-year-old daughter shucked her faith and no longer attends church. "Who am I to teach the Bible when my own flesh and blood doesn't buy into its message?" he laments.

A sense of deficiency also nags Jeff, who wasn't retained as youth director after a "trial year" under the new pastor; and Michael, who was once again snubbed for a promotion after a decade with a parachurch organization.

For every servant of Christ who demonstrates resiliency in response to failure there's another who flounders, so numbed by disappointment or self-recrimination his motivation wanes and productivity sags. Many persons quit ministering altogether. One explanation for such a devastating effect is spiritual warfare. Satan tries to exploit our mistakes and disappointments, hoping to derail current projects and hinder future endeavors for the Lord. In *The Screwtape Letters*, C. S. Lewis describes one of Satan's favorite strategies for impeding the spiritual growth and usefulness of Christians: get them to become preoccupied with their failures; from then on, his battle is won.

Shifting our focus away from ourselves and our inadequacies requires delving into God's Word. When we take missteps or don't reach our goals, what biblical perspectives can reinvigorate passion for the tasks he assigns? What truths furnish hope that God still uses folks after they've botched things or come up short?

I'll address those questions through the story of a Bible character who knew what it was like to take one step forward, two steps back.

On the Rebound

John Mark, younger cousin of Barnabas, resided with his mother in first-century Jerusalem. Church leaders often used their large house for prayer meetings (Acts 12:12). On their first missionary journey, Paul and Barnabas took Mark along as their assistant. Perhaps his primary role was to keep a written record of their forays into areas unreached by the gospel.

Over a decade later, Paul cited Mark among his co-laborers for the gospel (Col. 4:10; Philem. 24). Peter's affection for Mark became so pronounced that he referred to him as "son." They worked side by side for a while in Rome (1 Pet. 5:13). Mark's paramount achievement, the second Gospel of the New Testament, was the first written record of Jesus' life and ministry. According to Eusebius, a church historian, Mark topped off his vocational ministry career by establishing churches in Alexandria, Egypt.[1]

So far, it sounds like John Mark earned a page in the first-century edition of *Who's Who*. But as explained in a treatment of Barnabas in Chapter Five, there's also a dark episode in Mark's story.

Not far into the first missionary journey, Mark deserted Paul and Barnabas in Pamphylia, returning to the more comfortable confines of his home town (Acts 13:13). There's no explanation for his abrupt departure. Yet we know he didn't leave with the blessing of team members. Later, as the Acts narrative unfolded, Paul suggested a second trip to follow-up on churches started the first time around. Barnabas wanted John Mark to accompany them again. Paul's adamant refusal demonstrated his grievance toward Mark's previous abandonment of the team. He "kept insisting that they should not take him along who had deserted them in Pamphylia and had not gone with them to the work" (Acts 15:38). A vitriolic disagreement ensued between Paul and Barnabas, severing their partnership. Paul replaced Barnabas with Silas.

If we were to let down the most recognized and respected Christian leader of our era, how would *we* feel? If our immaturity or mistake resulted in his refusal to affiliate with us, could we muster the determination to press on? If what we did generated conflict and split up a team of workers, could we sleep at night?

Ah, but Mark's lapse was only a single episode in his life's script, not its climax. As I've already suggested, he finished far better than he started.

I've already noted how, after more than a decade of silence, Paul recognized Mark's contributions in two separate letters, and served as Peter's sidekick. But the primary indicator that Mark restored his tarnished reputation was seen in a gratifying tribute Paul paid him not long before the apostle's death. After asking Timothy to visit him in prison, Paul added, "Pick up Mark and bring him with you, *for he is useful to me for service*" (2 Tim. 4:11, emphasis mine).

Previously lambasted by Paul, now recruited by him. Once shunned by the early church's foremost leader, now sought after for companionship. Once doubted, now explicitly trusted with responsibility.

But John Mark's Gospel cemented his legacy. The Gospel of Mark reads like a PowerPoint presentation, showing through a rapid-fire succession of events who Jesus is and why he came. It's customary for Bible translators to select Mark's narrative first when they introduce the gospel to an unreached group of people.

No wonder I named my first son John Mark! I wanted a convincing way for him to remember that failure isn't final, that failures have a future.

What can we hoist from John Mark's story for our service in the twenty-first century? When it comes to work God delegated to us, why is it always too soon to quit?

The Bible doesn't say what happened in the years between Mark's desertion and his ministry comeback. But there's a reference in the Acts narrative revealing one way in which God redeems failure. For other perspectives that I believe inform this case study, I'll go elsewhere in Scripture.

Redeeming Failure

Reflecting on Mark's story and the probable dynamics of his rebounding from failure leads me to four conclusions:

1. *When we fail, we need a friend.* Barnabas' incarnation of God's forgiveness and love explains Mark's metamorphosis from deserter to profitable servant. After the breach with Paul, Barnabas took Mark to

Cyprus. As far as the biblical record is concerned, we don't hear from either man for an extended period of time. Barnabas' presence, and perhaps counsel, slowly implanted within Mark hope for future usefulness. Due to Barnabas' belief in him, Mark didn't keep nursing the wounds of Paul's rejection.

If you've failed, search high and low for a mentor whose presence and input will restore your passion for service. If you know someone floundering because of a gaffe, give him or her the gift of your time so that, through you, that person gets to know the God of the second chance who isn't put off by our fiascos. The other person will see God's acceptance mirrored in you. He or she will learn his grace by being graced.

2. *When we fail, we need a fresh awareness of God's grace.* When a mistake fits the category of sin, nothing helps short of running to the Lord, admitting our culpability, and taking him at his Word when he says, "If we confess our sins, He is faithful and just to forgive our sins and to cleanse us from all unrighteousness" (1 John 1:9).

If you're performance-oriented like me, forgiving yourself isn't easy. But as I studied the doctrine of the cross some time ago, it dawned on me that an unwillingness to forgive myself is tantamount to doctrinal heresy. It's the same as saying to God, "Your Son's death wasn't sufficient to deal with my sin. I must add to his sacrifice by heaping guilt on myself for what I did." How preposterous!

As a zealous Pharisee, Paul (then Saul) got it wrong concerning Jesus. He was in hot pursuit of anybody who thought Jesus was the Messiah. He "began ravaging the church, entering house after house, and dragging off men and women, he would put them in prison" (Acts 8:3). Paul kept "breathing threats and murder against the disciples of the Lord" (Acts 9:1). Yet after meeting Christ, there's no indication that self-reproach or guilt feelings badgered Paul's psyche. He took the Lord's offer of forgiveness at face value because he understood grace.

In 1 Timothy 1:12–17, Paul contrasted his zealous persecution of believers with the merciful intervention of Christ, explaining his about-face with these words: "the grace of our Lord was *more than abundant*" (emphasis mine). The italicized words literally mean "hyper in amount or intensity."

God more than matches overactive eruptions of our sin nature with grace that's every bit as hyper.

3. *Failure softens our hearts, weaning us from pride and self-sufficiency.* God hates a haughty spirit because, to use John Wesley's words, "All pride is idolatry."[2] A servant of Christ, once broken by failure, is far less likely to take the credit for any future successes. Perhaps the only thing that improves by breaking it is the human heart, for thereafter, it's open for the Lord's reconstructive work.

In the Old Testament, the failure of God's people in the wilderness was divine pedagogy. God contrived it in order to humble them and to expose the inherent disobedience embedded in their hearts. Moses said, "You shall remember all the way which the Lord your God has led you in the wilderness these forty years, that He might humble you, testing you, to know what was in your heart" (Deut. 8:2). John Mark's dereliction of duty and the hit his reputation took apparently resulted in a lifelong disposition toward humility and dependence. He, too, learned what was in his heart.

One of Charles Spurgeon's most capable pastoral trainees discovered the pedagogical value of failing. The young man, a gifted orator, could preach with the best of them, only he was enamored by his own giftedness. Once, with Spurgeon in the audience, the young man strutted to the pulpit as if he couldn't wait to start. Unexpectedly, in contrast to other sermons he'd delivered, he stammered and repeatedly struggled to express his thoughts. When he finished, the embarrassed speaker walked down from the pulpit with his head bowed and a dazed look on his face. Here's the essence of feedback given to him: "If you had gone up to the pulpit the way you came down, you would have come down the way you went up."[3]

4. *Failure and the subsequent encounter with God's grace tilt our focus away from ourselves, toward a preoccupation with the merciful nature of God.* Instead of brooding over what we've done to disappoint others and displease the Lord, we revel in what *he's* capable of doing for, in, and through persons who fall short.

No one's story illustrates this shift in focus better than John Newton's (1725–1807). When he worked on merchant ships as a young man, he couldn't get along with captains or shipmates. Profanity, heavy drinking, and gambling were routine. His resume included stints on ships transporting slaves to England.

After conversion to Christianity, he served as an Anglican pastor and wrote hymns, including "Amazing Grace." In his later years, he allied with William Wilberforce, whose painstaking work in Parliament led to abolition of the slave trade. From his deathbed, almost the last words Newton ever spoke were these: "I am a great sinner, but Christ is a great Savior."[4]

"But Christ . . ."

Those are hope-saturated words of contrast for all the John Marks of the world.

My wrap on this chapter is from James I. Packer, who echoes the need to preach to ourselves about God's character rather than focus on our foibles:

> If I found I had driven into a bog, I should know I had missed the road. But this knowledge would not be of much comfort if I then had to stand helpless watching the car sink and vanish: the damage would be done, and that would be that. Is it the same when a Christian wakes up to the fact that he has missed God's guidance and taken the wrong way? Is the damage irrevocable? Must he now be put off course for life? Thank God, no.
>
> Our God is a god who not merely restores, but takes up our mistakes and follies into His plan for us and brings good out of

them. This is part of the wonder of His gracious sovereignty. "I will restore to you the years that the locust has eaten. . . . " God makes not only the wrath of man to turn to His praise but the misadventures of Christians too.[5]

Dig Deeper

In this chapter, I alluded to the pedagogical value of failure for God's chosen people. Read Deuteronomy 8:1–20 and examine the text for answers to these questions:

What lessons did God want the people to learn about themselves? About him?

What is the inherent danger of success or blessings?

What repeated phrase—a posture of heart or spirit that's cited three times—represents the outcome God desires as a result of failing?

CHAPTER 14

The Power of Owning Up

When it comes to ministry, what instills feelings of unworthiness? What siphons off confidence that God can and will use you to make an eternal difference? What dilutes commitment to your tasks, producing a lethargic spirit rather than zeal for your calling?

For some servants, especially sensitive souls like me who don't readily apply God's grace to themselves, it's a keen awareness of their shortcomings: weaknesses of temperament, vulnerability to certain temptations, difficulty getting along with someone they love, inconsistency with spiritual disciplines, or a fragile ego. We teach about God's grace, yet badger ourselves over flaws that we believe disqualify us from making a significant impact for God.

I can't count the times over the years when, right before entering a classroom or pulpit, I've muttered, "Who am I to teach others?!" I've pictured angels elbowing each other, pointing accusing fingers at me, snickering at my feeble attempts to practice what I preach.

What reassurance I've received from the biblical perspective in this chapter!

Shortcomings in Christian living or ministry are harbingers of opportunity.[1] The pivot on which failure turns into usefulness is our response to it. We can react in a way that magnifies our influence and enhances our status as positive role models.

The response I'm referring to is *the power of owning up*: the beneficial effects of a soft heart toward God and a transparent approach toward people that readily acknowledges when we've blown it.

The best way to explain the concept is to illustrate it.

Transparent Teacher

Naomi taught a girls' middle school class at her church. She cultivated a close relationship with the girls, hosting them in her home and initiating service projects they did together. She also took preparation for her weekly Bible lesson seriously. That's the backdrop for a particular incident that proved formative for the girls.

On the way to their church campus on a Sunday morning, she and her husband engaged in a heated verbal exchange. Naomi called it "a knock-down, drag-out fight." They left the car in a huff without making things right between them. A few minutes into her lesson, Naomi fidgeted and put down her Bible. She described the argument, admitted that her attitude toward her husband had been unreasonable, and asked several of the girls to pray for her while she dealt with the Lord silently.

The last thing Naomi felt like was a good role model. But stop and analyze her actions and the potential effect on the girls. What did she model for them about Christian living? About teaching God's Word?

She demonstrated humility, a contrite heart toward sin, and the necessity of confession. Without the benefit of a Bible study on confession, the girls saw an embodiment of 1 John 1:8–9: "If we say we have no sin, we are deceiving ourselves and the truth is not in us. If we confess our sins, He is faithful and righteous to forgive our sins and to cleanse us from all unrighteousness." Naomi's forthright admission also receives God's favor: "To this one I will look, to him who is humble and contrite of spirit, and who trembles at My word" (Isa. 66:2).

By soliciting their prayers, Naomi displayed a reliance on other believers' support. She gave them an opportunity to experience Galatians 6:2: "Bear one another's burdens." The girls learned that others in the body of Christ can't help bear burdens that we don't disclose.

The girls observed authenticity concerning one's walk with God. They saw a flawed teacher, yet one who relied upon a flawless Savior. They viewed Naomi's weakness within the larger framework of the Lord's strength and forgiveness.

Naomi modeled a high view of teaching Scripture. She couldn't proceed with the lesson without a right heart before God. They learned from her that a vital component when serving God is heart readiness.

I'm not foisting my own conclusion onto the story. Naomi's disclosure deepened her bond with the girls. Her transparency and soft heart enhanced rather than diminished her credibility in their eyes.[2]

The second illustration I'll give of this concept hits closer to home. The spotlight shifts to the ministry of parenting.

A Parent's Mistake

On his seventh birthday, a half-dozen of my older son's friends cluttered our house for a party. During the festivities, I pulled Mark aside and expressed displeasure at how he was treating one of his guests. Instead of heeding my advice, as he usually did, he talked back to me. Normally, the consequence for such behavior was a spanking. But with his friends crowded around, I let his remark slide. Nor did I address his disrespectful behavior after the party. Perhaps I was afraid that meting out discipline would spoil his birthday.

The next day, I realized I had been too soft on Mark. I resolved not to let him off the hook the next time he misbehaved. I didn't want him to get the idea that he could act disrespectfully and get away with it. In retrospect, to compensate for the day before, perhaps I was looking for an opportunity to punish him.

Later that following day, I walked into the house as Mark and his younger brother, Stephen, scuffled in the hallway outside their rooms. In a knee-jerk reaction, I pulled Mark from the fracas and took him to his room, figuring he had been picking on Stephen. We had a strict rule against starting a fight. Over Mark's strong protest, I began spanking him. That's when the door to Mark's room flew open.

"You're punishing the wrong boy," my wife announced. "Stephen just told me that he jumped on Mark. Mark was only trying to fend off Stephen's blows."

"That's what I was trying to tell you!" Mark said between sobs.

Their words crushed me. I had never disciplined my sons unjustly nor abused them in any way. Had I damaged Mark's sensitive spirit? Had I driven a wedge between us that would be difficult to dislodge? Would he forgive me?

I slumped to the floor beside his bed, tears streaming from my eyes. "I'm sorry," I said to Mark. "I'll never punish you again before listening to you. Please forgive me." With Mark by my side, I knelt by his bed, confessed my sin to the Lord, and cried out for the wisdom I needed as a dad. That evening, as I tucked Mark into bed, I repeated my plea for forgiveness. He hugged me and assured me that things were okay between us.

A week after my gaffe, I still goaded myself for my reprehensible behavior. Over breakfast with a friend, I recounted the incident. His reaction surprised me.

"What a positive role model you were to your son!" He exclaimed.

"What do you mean?" I replied. "How in the world could an unjust spanking cast me as a positive role model?"

"All you remember is your failure," countered my friend. "But I believe your brokenness overshadowed your mistake. You weren't too proud to admit you failed. What Mark will remember most is a dad who apologized to him through tears, who slumped to his knees and confessed to God with a contrite spirit. *What you modeled for him is how to handle sin."*

Pattern, Not Perfection

Modeling is the primary avenue of a leader's influence. When it comes to Christian values, more is caught than taught. When it comes to teaching, Jesus said that we communicate *likeness*, not just Bible content: "A pupil is not above his teacher; but everyone, after he has been fully trained, will be like his teacher" (Luke 6:40). Paul urged Timothy and Titus to "show yourself an example" to church members in Ephesus and Crete (1 Tim. 4:12, Tit. 2:7).

From the Greek word translated "example," we derive the term "type." I'm old enough to remember using a typewriter. When I pecked on the key for the letter "g," the typeset pressed the ink ribbon against the paper, leaving an imprint of the "g." In Paul's day, the word described a mark left by a blow to the body. The black eye an assailant gave his victim was a *tupos.*

Inevitably, leaders, teachers, and parents leave a mark on others. We strive to leave a positive impression through pristine character and resilient faith. But as Naomi's story and mine demonstrate, even when we fall short, there's potential for constructive impact.

We can't model perfection, but we can exhibit the authentic process of following Christ in a fallen world. The same Paul who set high standards for Timothy and Titus, who urged folks to follow his own example (Phil. 3:17; 4:9), also called himself the chief of sinners (1 Tim. 1:15). He realized that serving as a positive role model required not a life free from sin, but an overall pattern of godliness, or a Godward trajectory over time. That's why he encouraged readers to live "according to the *pattern* we gave you" (Phil. 3:17, emphasis mine).

So long as we live authentically before God and others, not hiding our shortcomings or pretending we're strong when we aren't . . .

So long as we view our weaknesses within the framework of God's strength and grace . . .

We'll experience the ironic, hope-inspiring truth that our response to failure may have a positive impact on others.

I'll close with Larry Richard's take on the value of openness among those who serve the Lord.

Self-revelation is a strength, not a weakness, in spiritual leadership. The reasons for this are rooted in theology: First, we are to be examples not of perfection, but of a process. Second, we are to reflect the gospel. And the gospel is not "accept Christ and become perfect." The gospel is Jesus saying, "Without me you can do nothing!" (John 15:5). If we misrepresent ourselves as so "strong" that we do not need Jesus, we misrepresent the gospel of God's grace.

The Gospel is God's promise that when we accept our weakness and inadequacy, He will provide His supernatural power and vitality. When we pretend to be something we aren't, we rob God of the glory that is His alone for the growth and change that is taking place in our personalities. When I am willing to reveal my weaknesses to others, then they may see the power of Christ as He works to overcome them. Then I demonstrate—not deny—the Gospel.

None of this detracts in any way from the leader's responsibility to be a good example in godliness. But it does cut us off from being hypocritical. It eliminates the need to pretend whenever we hurt. In sharing ourselves, in being real with others, they may well see our weakness . . . but they will also see Jesus' strength! And it will be encouraging that the transformation Jesus has been working in us can be worked in them as well.[3]

Dig Deeper

Think of a time when you observed a Christian worker who demonstrated a soft heart in response to a mistake, who readily apologized or owned up to failure.

How did this person's response illustrate "the power of owning up"?

What positive virtues or traits did this person model for others?

How did this person's contrite response affect your attitude toward him or her?

Owning up to failure always results in God's favor. And those who observe us learn the kind of response that pleases God.

CHAPTER 15

THE MINISTRY OF PAIN

WOULDN'T IT BE GREAT IF YOU BURNED YOUR HAND ON A SCALDING POT, YET DIDN'T FEEL A THING? IF YOU FELL OFF a ladder when cleaning your roof, landing with a thud on your arm, without one iota of pain? If you accidently whacked your thumb with a hammer, yet it didn't throb?

No, it wouldn't.

Bob and Christine Waters, from Great Britain, developed a far different take on pain. Their three children were born with a rare physical malady: congenital analgesia, an insensitivity to physical pain. Instead of a reason to celebrate, it's actually a curse.

When they were toddlers, their kids bit off the tips of their fingers and tongues, permanently scarred themselves with self-imposed cuts, severely burned their hands, and broke numerous bones. Before one of their daughters reached her second birthday, she broke her right leg five times. Another child suffered from a chronic nosebleed, a result of repeatedly banging her face on the floor. Bob and Christine learned the hard way that *pain is a friend, not a foe.* It's a built-in means of warning us and protecting us from a lot worse physical calamity.[1]

For God's people, pain isn't necessarily an enemy in other realms of life, either. Though no one puts out a welcome mat for affliction, the benefits often outweigh the unpleasantness. Scripture attests that "many are the afflictions of the righteous" (Ps. 34:19). James mirrors the teaching of a number of biblical authors when he cites the faith-testing, character-building outcomes of trials (James 1:2–4).

My aim isn't to explore a theology of suffering. Nor is it to elaborate on the subject of pain for God's people in general. I'm addressing folks with a passion to serve the Lord who crave to make an eternal difference with their lives. And here's the single insight around which I'm framing this chapter: *what hurts us packs the potential to enlarge the borders of our influence for Christ.*

If you and I brainstormed together for ways to increase the fruitfulness of our lives, our list of ideas would include catalysts for enhanced productivity, such as

- deepening our knowledge of God's Word,
- interceding more fervently for persons we serve or want to reach,
- reading books from experienced leaders who think incisively and creatively about ministry,
- attending conferences for professional development, and
- finding a mentor with wisdom to tap into.

Painful experiences probably wouldn't make the list. Yet the inevitable hurts of living in a fallen world are pregnant with ministry potential. The late Baptist pastor Ronald Dunn went so far as to say, "Your greatest area of usefulness for Christ may stem from your greatest area of pain."[2]

What did he mean? How can physical setbacks, heartache, flaws of temperament, or mistreatment extend the perimeters of our influence and augment our impact on others?

Addressing those questions requires excavating the biblical roots of this concept.

Receiving and Giving Comfort

When Jesus appeared to the zealous Pharisee, Saul, he disclosed that Saul's new commission as an apostle would involve large-scale suffering (Acts 9:15–16). Long before his martyrdom, the evangelist and church planter who became known as Paul endured hunger, sleepless nights, imprisonments, multiple beatings with rods, stoning, five assaults with whips totaling 195 lashes, shipwreck, and constant threats from foes of the gospel (2 Cor. 11:23–28). To those external hardships, add the pressure of concern for churches he started, especially the attempts of false teachers to undermine the purity of the gospel.

Paul's litany of afflictions serves as the backdrop to 2 Corinthians 1:3–11. As you peruse this passage, note the initial despair in response to the difficulties, then zero in on ultimate outcomes of his pain. What redemptive results can you identify?

> Blessed *be* the God and Father of our Lord Jesus Christ, the Father of mercies and God of all comfort, who comforts us in all our affliction so that we will be able to comfort those who are in any affliction with the comfort with which we ourselves are comforted by God. For just as the sufferings of Christ are ours in abundance, so also our comfort is abundant through Christ. But if we are afflicted, it is for your comfort and salvation; or if we are comforted, it is for your comfort, which is effective in the patient enduring of the same sufferings which we also suffer; and our hope for you is firmly grounded, knowing that as you are sharers of our sufferings, so also you are sharers of our comfort.
>
> For we do not want you to be unaware, brethren, of our affliction which came *to us* in Asia, that we were burdened

excessively, beyond our strength, so that we despaired even of life; indeed, we had the sentence of death within ourselves so that we would not trust in ourselves, but in God who raises the dead; who delivered us from so great a *peril of* death, and will deliver *us*, He on whom we have set our hope. And He will yet deliver us, you also joining in helping us through your prayers, so that thanks may be given by many persons on our behalf for the favor bestowed on us through *the prayers of* many.

The returns for Paul included a weaning from self-reliance, a deeper trust in the Lord's character, plus a greater capacity to help others who hurt. It's the last outcome I want to put the spotlight on.

Absorb the emphasis on Paul's expanded ability to empathize with and comfort others. God sustained Paul "so that we may be able to comfort those who are in any affliction with the comfort with which we ourselves are comforted by God" (v. 4). Because he suffered abundantly, "so also our comfort is abundant through Christ" (v. 5). He even went so far as to say that "if we are afflicted, it is for your comfort and salvation" (v. 6).

In the crucible of suffering, Paul had observed the Lord intervening on his behalf, sparing his life on multiple occasions so he could keep serving. When he wasn't spared from difficulty, Paul experienced the peaceful presence of God's Spirit, who instilled contentment in the midst of adversity (Phil. 4:11; Acts 16:22–25). Whether divine intervention altered his circumstances or transformed him on the inside, Paul discovered experientially what God can do for a person. His own stressors and the initial despondency they fostered ramped up his compassion for hurting folks. His identification with others' pain enabled him to heed his own advice to "rejoice with those who rejoice, and weep with those who weep" (Rom. 12:15).

I know of a pastor so forlorn that he considered suicide while strolling alone on a beach. He felt he couldn't take any more hard knocks. He couldn't imagine how things would get any better.

Then a worried friend showed up at the beach. The friend didn't condemn his depressed companion for lack of faith, nor did he dish out superficial solutions. Instead, he walked alongside the hurting person, listened to him vent, told him he loved him, and prayed for him.

The friend's gift of presence incarnated God's love and spawned hope in the despondent leader. To use the pastor's own words, "My life started coming together again." As it turns out, his comforter had experienced a rough patch in his own life and knew first-hand the sustaining power of God's Spirit, and how God fleshes out concern for us through others in the body of Christ. This comforter's own broken heart had kept him from a self-righteous, judgmental attitude. Instead of offering glib, snap-out-of-it advice, he lifted the rocks off his Christian brother's chest.

This expanded ministry of Paul's pain hinged, at least in part, on his willingness to talk or to write about it. He referred to his affliction in Asia, the devastating effects on his spirit, and shared how deeper faith in God and less reliance on himself resulted (2 Cor. 1:8–9). What expedites our ability to help hurting people isn't merely our own episodes of pain, coupled with experiencing some form of God's comfort. It's our willingness to self-reveal, to explain how God became more real and precious to us during the distress, disclosing what he did for us, planting a seed of hope in others who need a fresh infusion of God's grace. It's okay if our transparency depicts us as weak and needy, so long as what we say portrays the Lord as strong and compassionate.

Yet the truth that our pain can reap eternal dividends doesn't depend exclusively on our actions or self-disclosures. On his own, God can salvage ultimate good from our setbacks.

A Redemptive Purpose

When God permits, or perhaps designs, suffering in the lives of his servants, he has a bigger picture in mind than merely what's happening to us. Foremost in his thinking is his plan of redemption and the spread of the gospel, not our own repose or gratification.

The Apostle Paul's life offers a case in point. In Philippi, authorities arrested him and Silas, beat them with rods, and fastened their feet in the stocks. Their tribulation eventually resulted in the salvation of the jailor and his household (Acts 16:22–33). Years later, a fruit of Paul's first imprisonment in Rome was the impetus it gave to other believers who took up the slack. His confinement spurred them to preach in places where Paul couldn't go, prompting Paul to write, "My circumstances have turned out for the greater progress of the gospel" (Phil. 1:12).

The eighteenth century provides another riveting example of how God sovereignly redeems our pain for a greater purpose.

David Brainerd (1718–1747) took the gospel of Christ to Indians in Massachusetts, Pennsylvania, and New Jersey, often living alone with sparse food rations and exposure to cold. Extremely melancholy in temperament, Brainerd endured long episodes of joylessness, often slinking into despair over awareness of his sin or over an incapacity to feel more love for the people he was trying to reach. Physical frailty accompanied his psychological anguish. He died of tuberculosis before his thirtieth birthday.

Despite the pendulum swings in his spirit and tendency toward morbid introspection, Brainerd sensed a strong sense of call to the Indians. Time and again he devoted entire days to fasting and prayer for their salvation. A couple years after launching missionary work among them, in 1845, God's Spirit brought a spiritual awakening in New Jersey. Within a year of the awakening, the church Brainerd started numbered 130.

Brainerd kept a diary in which he described bouts of despondency, disclosed his consciousness of sin in light of God's holiness, and recounted efforts to evangelize the Indians. Its pages teem with honest self-disclosure as well as desperate dependence on God for physical and emotional sustenance. Twenty-two places in his diary, he expressed a yearning for death as an escape from his misery. Yet he persisted in proclaiming Christ, even when his own temperamental makeup eclipsed his ability to experience the joy inherent in the gospel. One entry revealed his acceptance of weakness and deeply-entrenched desire to finish well: "Oh, for more of God in my soul! Oh, this pleasing pain! It makes my soul press after God. . . . Oh, that I might never loiter on my heavenly journey."[3]

During his lifetime, Brainerd's most potent influence was on pastor and theologian Jonathan Edwards, in whose house Brainerd died. Edwards considered the time with Brainerd a "gracious dispensation of Providence. . . . [To] see his dying behavior, to hear his dying speeches, to receive his dying counsel, and to have the benefit of his dying prayers."[4]

Yet after his death, the fruit of Brainerd's life multiplied exponentially. In 1749, Edwards took the diaries and published them as *Life of Brainerd*, a book that's never been out of print. Renowned missionaries and leaders galvanized by Brainerd's story include John Wesley, Henry Martyn, William Carey, Robert Murray McCheyne, David Livingstone, Andrew Murray, and Jim Elliot. According to John Piper, "The impact of Brainerd on the church has been incalculable. Beyond all the famous missionaries who tell us that they have been sustained and inspired . . . how many countless other unknown faithful servants must there be who have found from Brainerd's testimony the encouragement and strength to press on."[5]

The borders of Brainerd's impact weren't expanded *in spite of* his emotional and physical afflictions, but *because of* them. His story has resonated with so many servants over the years because when push comes to shove, they, too, wrestle with sinful propensities, episodes of depression, and physical frailties. They believe they are candidates for the same divine grace they observe in Brainerd's life. John Piper, he himself buoyed by Brainerd's story, offers this apt summary statement: "Brainerd's life is a vivid, powerful testimony to the truth that God can and does use weak, sick, discouraged, beat-down, lonely, struggling saints who cry to him day and night to accomplish amazing things for his glory."[6]

Now, to the explanation and illustration of the "pain enhances ministry" concept, let's add application to our present lives.

So What?

Since our hurts pack the potential to expand our ministry, what are the implications for the way we think about them and how we respond? Here's the fallout of this perspective for me.

1. Awareness that others may receive help from my affliction, that God can capitalize on it for a redemptive outcome, assuages my grief.

2. How I pray changes. I still plead with God to alleviate the pain, to alter the burdensome circumstance or heal my damaged emotions, but I include requests for him to utilize my experience for a greater good. I not only ask him to deepen my faith and purify my character, but to bless others somehow and to boost his reputation as a result. More than once, with tears streaming down my cheeks, I've cried, "Lord, don't waste my pain!"

3. I weave my stories of pain into my conversations and teaching opportunities. So long as I don't break confidences or disparage anyone else in the process, I mention my struggles, what God teaches me through them, and how he dispensed comfort. Like Paul in 2 Corinthians 1, I strive to pass along the help I've received from God during trials.

For instance, I'll describe in stark detail the symptoms of a depressive episode. Then I explain the Bible verses that reassured me of God's presence and concern. I'll mention the encouragement of Christian friends God sent my way. And I'll tell how God enabled me for ministry tasks that I didn't feel like doing. He gets glory and others receive hope.

As Alan Nelson puts it in *Embracing Brokenness*, "Pain does not seem quite so bad when it appears to serve a purpose."[7]

Dig Deeper

In *The Hidden Smile of God* (Crossway Books, 2001), John Piper profiles three historical figures who illustrate the enhancement of ministry through pain. Subtitled *The Fruit of Affliction in the Lives of John Bunyan, William Cowper, and David Brainerd,* Piper's book offers two case studies involving a proclivity for emotional or temperamental malaise and another featuring severe persecution from without. Their stories strengthen my soul and illustrate the fruit of affliction far more comprehensively than I do in this chapter.

After you read this book, ponder these questions: which historical profile encourages you most? Why? In what sense does the life of each man reveal "the *hidden* smile of God"?

CHAPTER 16

THE TRACKS OF YOUR TEARS

As a Bible study leader, preacher, or mentor, has a comforting truth ever drenched your heart to such an extent that, while communicating it to others, tears streaked down your cheeks? Were you embarrassed? Did you apologize for your lack of self-control?

Does heartbreak over people without Christ or over persons with grievous burdens ever evoke in you fits of weeping? When that happens, do you silently reprove yourself for being emotionally frail or too sentimental, figuring you could serve them and God more efficiently if only you were more reserved, less demonstrative?

Is your affective domain so hyperactive that you weep at the slightest provocation, and conclude you're too brittle to fill some ministry positions for which you're otherwise gifted?

When push comes to shove, do you think crying in public is incompatible with strong leadership? That sobbing is mutually exclusive with spirituality? That tears are incongruent with trusting God?

If you reply yes to any of those inquiries, that's a reason to keep reading. If you equate your sensitive spirit with weakness or immaturity, the next few pages will reassure you. God's view on tears is often at odds with our own. And if you're prone to weeping, you'll discover that you keep very good company. Many towering personalities from the Bible were known for tear-stained faces.

Misty-Eyed Leaders

What follows are but a few of the heroic biblical figures whose tears made rivulets down their cheeks. As you peruse these brief profiles, look for *why* they wept.

Inconsolable

The prophet Isaiah couldn't stomach God's forecast of judgment for his wayward people: "Let me weep bitterly, do not try to comfort me concerning the destruction of the daughter of my people" (Isa. 22:4). Even God's pronouncement of devastation for the inhabitants of Moab evoked a similar response in Isaiah: "I will weep bitterly for Jazer, for the vine of Sibmah; I will drench you with my tears, O Heshbon and Elealeh" (Isa. 16:9).

Weeping Prophet

When he conveyed God's warning of dire consequences for Judah's rebellion, Jeremiah admitted, "If you will not listen to it, my soul will sob in secret for *such* pride; and my eyes will bitterly weep and flow down with tears, because the flock of the LORD has been taken captive" (Jer. 13:17). When he observed the sorrows in Zion inflicted by God's discipline, he lamented, "For these things I weep; my eyes run down with water; because far from me is a comforter . . . my children are desolate because the enemy has prevailed" (Lam. 1:16).

Responsive to Revelation

When Josiah took over the reins of the nation, Judah was in the throes of rampant idolatry and spiritual decay. When a priest read aloud to Josiah a long-lost copy of the Law, the stark contrast between God's expectations and the nation's moral climate broke his heart, resulting in a spate of top-down policies for spiritual reform. A prophetess divulged God's opinion of Josiah's initial response to the Law: "Because your heart was tender and you humbled yourself before God when you heard His words against this place and against its inhabitants, and *because* you humbled yourself before Me, tore your clothes and wept before Me, I truly have heard you" (2 Chron. 34:27).

Prostrated Priest

Ezra couldn't tolerate blatant sin among God's people, such as marrying foreigners. "I tore my garment . . . pulled some of the hair from my head and my beard, and sat down appalled" (Ezra 9:3). According to Ezra 10:1, he "was praying and making confession, weeping and prostrating himself before the house of God."

Newsworthy Intercession

Nehemiah, the cupbearer to the Babylonian king, received negative news from the remnant who had returned to Jerusalem after seventy years of captivity. The city wall was rubble, the residents vulnerable to attack and the object of derision from foes. Nehemiah felt burdened for their safety and he was distraught because God's glory was entwined with the fate of his people. Before he knew God would lead him to superintend the construction of the wall, here's how Nehemiah responded to the report: "I sat down and wept and mourned for days; and I was fasting and praying before the God of heaven" (Neh. 1:4).

Brash, Then Broken

Brazen, impulsive, but die-hard in his allegiance, Peter boasted that he would stay loyal to Jesus (Mark 14:29). Yet that same evening, to save his own skin, three times he denied knowing the Lord. When he remembered Jesus' prediction of the triad of disavowals, Peter "wept bitterly" over his failure (Matt. 26:75).

Apostolic Anguish

Referring to his prior ministry in Ephesus, Paul told the church elders, "Night and day for a period of three years I did not cease to admonish each one of you with tears" (Acts 20:31). Perhaps teardrops also stained the parchment on which he penned letters. Citing a moral failure in the church at Corinth that he addressed in a previous letter, Paul said, "Out of much affliction and anguish of heart I wrote to you with many tears; not so that you would be made sorrowful, but that you might know the love which I have especially for you" (2 Cor. 2:4).

A Savior's Sobs

Jesus wasn't immune to public displays of emotion. Despite knowing his plan to resurrect Lazarus, he nonetheless wept in front of onlookers when he observed the crying and grief of Lazarus' sister (John 11:33–36). Our Savior wept as he approached Jerusalem, brokenhearted over future judgment that would ravish the city (Luke 19:41–44). Eruptions of tears also came when he prayed prior to the crucifixion: "In the days of His flesh, He offered up both prayers and supplications with loud crying and tears to the One able to save Him from death" (Heb. 5:7).

Conclusions about Crying

What insights can we hoist from the biblical record of tenderhearted leaders? Though my intent in this chapter is to encourage sensitive souls by showing God's take on their tears, allow His Spirit to challenge you here as well.

1. *The crying of servants in Scripture wasn't restricted to emotionally fragile persons with a melancholy temperament.* Nehemiah and Paul were tough-as-nails, in-your-face leaders who consistently demonstrated choleric traits. It's a gross misconception to view weeping as the proclivity of a temperament that's in need of repair.

2. *The grief that sin generates in God's heart and the painful consequences of sin on others should hurt us.* Through Joel, God conveyed his expectations for spiritual leaders: "Let the priests, the Lord's ministers, weep between the porch and the altar, and let them say, 'Spare Your people, O LORD'" (Joel 2:17).

Over twenty-five years ago, evangelist Leonard Ravenhill provided a more contemporary example of a leader hurt by the sin and spiritual inertia of God's people. The renowned author of *Why Revival Tarries*[1] was the subject of a radio interview by David Mains on a Chapel of the Air broadcast. Ravenhill mentioned the numerous local churches where he had been guest speaker over the years. He regretted a frivolous attitude among his hosts toward the worship of God and the preaching of his Word. When pastors and elders or deacons gathered in the church office with Ravenhill prior to the service, they often told jokes or congratulated each other for whose team won the previous day. Then they typically offered a perfunctory prayer for the blessing of Ravenhill's message. He saw little grief over spiritual apathy in churches and almost no prevailing prayer concerning the eternal destinies of persons in the pews. Recalling the pattern of levity he sensed among leaders spawned tears in Ravenhill during the interview—not subdued sniffing or soft whimpering, but loud bawling so intense that his body convulsed. Moments later, when he regained a modicum of composure, his next words were, "And I'm afraid this hurts God!"

3. *God endorses tears among his servants for their own sins as well.* Like Peter, perhaps a keen awareness of our own penchant to fail the Lord will keep us humble when he starts using us in ministry. The hinge on which Peter's effectiveness turned was this heartache over letting Jesus down.

Time and again throughout Scripture, God mandates a tender-hearted response to our sins. Perhaps Joel 2:12–13 is the most riveting example: "Return to Me with all your heart, and with fasting, weeping and mourning; and rend your heart and not your garments." James gave similar counsel to young Jewish believers who tried to exploit God's grace with loathsome behavior. What he said would sound out of place, politically incorrect, in most church pulpits: "Be miserable and mourn and weep; let your laughter be turned into mourning and your joy to gloom" (James 4:9).

Back in 1974, Joseph Bayly wrote a captivating magazine column titled "Why Don't Sinners Cry Anymore?" His concern over the absence of brokenness and tears is a needed corrective for today's spiritual lethargy:

> British thinker-preacher Martyn Lloyd-Jones once commented that people no longer weep at evangelistic meetings. They laugh, he said, they come happily to the front, but they don't mourn over their sins. . . .
>
> Godly sorrow for sin that leads to repentance is almost totally absent from our preaching and from our lives. The one who enters the kingdom without repentance hardly finds need for it as a resident. We have lost the ability to say "I'm sorry" to God and to one another. We have lost it as persons and we have lost it in our churches and we have lost it as a nation. . . .
>
> Joseph C. Macaulay told of a visit to the Herbrides Islands some years ago, when revival was going on. On his way to church, where he was to preach, Dr. Macaulay heard a man sobbing in a cottage as he passed.
>
> "What's that?" he asked his companion.
>
> "That's John. He's on his way to God. He'll come through," was the reply.[2]

4. *Teary eyes caused by exposure to his Word pleases God.* I once came across an anonymous remark on the importance of a writer feeling

the impact of what he or she was expressing to others: "No tears in the writer, no tears in the reader." That also applies to those who teach or preach. *How does truth we communicate affect us?*

Robert Murray McCheyne's preaching and evangelistic zeal sparked a Scottish revival in the 1830s to 1840s. Known for his staunch devotional life, he pledged not to see the face of man each day until, through prayer and Bible reading, he saw the face of God. He consistently filtered what he preached through his own life, often generating tears long before he reached the pulpit.

After McCheyne died of illness at age thirty, a visitor to his church, enamored by McCheyne's sterling reputation, asked the caretaker for information on his study habits and preaching style. The sexton took the guest to McCheyne's study where the pastor had applied God's Word to his own heart before polishing messages for the congregation. Pointing to McCheyne's desk, he said, "Sit down. Now put your hands over your face. Now let the tears fall—this is the way my master studied."[3]

Next, the sexton took him into the sanctuary and coaxed the visitor into the pulpit. "Lean over, way over, and stretch out your hands towards the congregation. Now let the tears fall. That is the way my master preached."

5. The final conclusion that I culled from the Scripture search is succinct but sobering. *Since Jesus cried, and one of God the Father's goals for us is "to become conformed to the image of His Son" (Rom. 8:29), perhaps dry eyes should embarrass us more than a deluge of tears.*

Steely Resolve

R. A. Torrey (1856–1928), a reputable Christian leader in the Chicago area, told the story of a businessman who volunteered at an inner-city rescue mission. Colonel Clark spoke almost every night of the week to the motley crowd of drunkards, thieves, and gamblers. Despite a dull, rambling preaching style, men listened to Clark, riveted. Clark led many men to Christ. The destitute men responded far more positively to Clark than they did to the polished messages of highly-trained guest pastors such as Torrey himself.

According to Torrey, Clark's secret was his habit of weeping when he spoke or made an evangelistic appeal. The men, who had shed more than their fair share of tears over their brokenness, saw Clark's sobbing as proof that he loved them. During his early years at the mission, Clark felt ashamed of his wailing in front of the men. He steeled his heart, determined not to lose his composure when he shared the gospel. But ,a loss of power accompanied the absence of weeping. Responsiveness among the men dried up. Before long, Clark got alone with God and pleaded, "Oh God, give me back my tears!"[4]

Closing Perspectives

Allow me to qualify my commendation of weeping. Some folks cry because they need emotional healing. Due to tragedy, abuse, or other complex psychological factors, they are "broken in the wrong places." For such persons, God often dispenses his grace through a caring community, a professional counselor, and in some cases, medical intervention.

There's also a type of weeping that's abhorrent to God. I call it the "tears of a sentimentalist," whose sorrow is worldly rather than godly. It's when we cry out to God over painful consequences of sin, yet we're unwilling to disengage from that sin. It's when we complain over how God is treating us, when all the while he's striving to get our attention through the unpleasant circumstances. Malachi 2:13-14 depicts this form of self-centered sorrow:

> You cover the altar of the LORD with your tears, with weeping and with groaning, because He no longer regards the offering or accepts *it with* favor from your hand. Yet you say, "For what reason?" Because the LORD has been a witness between you and the wife of your youth, against whom you have dealt treacherously, though she is your companion and your wife by covenant.

Yet for the most part, God has a soft spot for people who weep. A propensity to cry may reveal a tender heart toward God and others. Tears may reflect brokenheartedness over the consequences of sin people face or over the marring sin causes God's reputation. When we expose ourselves to God's Word, weeping may show a receptivity to both the Holy Spirit's conviction and his comfort.

If you cry for the right reasons, stop apologizing. Stop equating your tears with instability or immaturity. Stop being so proud that you don't want others to see what's in your heart. Stop thinking that a sensitive spirit disqualifies you from service.

If you're called to vocational Christian ministry, add "prone to weep" to the credentials on your résumé. And if you almost never cry, perhaps it's time to follow Colonel Clark's lead and ask the Lord for more tears.

Dig Deeper

Tears caused by the pain of tragic loss, irreconcilable relationships, mistreatment, or other hurts were outside the domain of this chapter. But if you've cried recently for personal reasons that don't fit the coverage of preceding pages, cling to the hope-generating promise of Revelation 21:4. When God suspends this realm of time and space and we're enjoying a new heaven and earth, "He will wipe away every tear from their eyes; and there will no longer be *any* death; there will no longer be *any* mourning, or crying, or pain."

The very day I'm writing this I've wept over my sin, over a relative who's alienated from God, and over a brief but smothering episode of depression. But Revelation 21:4 pierced my darkness with a ray of light. I even cracked a smile.

Part Three

When You Don't See Results

A severe test of a worker's faith is doubt concerning fruitfulness. What biblical insights inform us when efforts appear futile? Why does the Lord allow times of barrenness? The biblical insights in the following chapters will cultivate perseverance.

CHAPTER 17

Reaping
What You Sow

FOR OVER TWENTY YEARS I'VE PRAYED FOR A CLOSE RELATIVE TO RETURN TO CHRIST. SO FAR, DESPITE A WARM relationship between us, there's no movement on his part toward faith in Christ or the church.

———— ⇝ ————

A pastor I know has led the same congregation for over a decade. He receives numerous compliments for his preaching, yet he admits feeling ambivalent about its effects. "I don't see noticeable life change among members," he remarks. "I wonder if all the study and energy that goes into preaching make any real difference."

———— ⇝ ————

Tears cascaded down Jerry's red cheeks. His chin quivered, making it difficult to talk. "I feel like a failure," he stammered. "Did I waste all those years in seminary? I'm wondering if God called me to vocational ministry, after all."

What creates Jerry's perplexity is the inability to land a church position since graduating two years ago. Despite interviews with three churches and two parachurch organizations, he languishes in a low-level administrative job, frustrated because his potential remains untapped, his calling unfulfilled. "I just want someone to want me," he laments.

To those scenarios, add the mentor who met weekly with a young man for months, only to see his protégé leave the church and shuck his commitment to Christ. And the lady whose attempts at personal evangelism are met with a chilly reception. Include the young mother whose speaking ministry has been curtailed by the birth of a special-needs child, or the missions recruiter whose trips to several Christian colleges haven't landed a prospective candidate.

In John 15, Jesus identified his followers as branches who are expected to bear fruit. But it's unsettling when the branches appear bare, when God withholds his blessing, when results seem nonexistent.

What biblical insights can fuel faith and instill resilience for the barren times?

That's the question I address in the next eight chapters. God's Word is far from mute on the subject. I'll introduce you to the Bible passages and theological perspectives that rejuvenate me when I'm disillusioned or I'm questioning the outcomes of my efforts. I'll hoist the first faith-enhancing answer from an agricultural analogy penned by the apostle Paul.

Planting Seeds

Paul's familiar metaphor about sowing and reaping informs us during phases of ministry that appear unproductive.

> The one who is taught the word is to share all good things with the one who teaches *him*. Do not be deceived, God is not mocked; for whatever a man sows, this he will also reap. For

the one who sows to his own flesh will from the flesh reap corruption, but the one who sows to the Spirit will from the Spirit
reap eternal life. Let us not lose heart in doing good, for in due
time we will reap if we do not grow weary. So then, while we
have opportunity, let us do good to all people, and especially
to those who are of the household of the faith. (Gal. 6:6–10)

When we put an ear to this passage, what do we hear? Whether we "sow
to the flesh" through indulgence in sin or "sow to the Spirit" through
contributions to what's eternal, Paul insists that our actions foster consequences. Most folks associate the sow-reap principle with the painful
effects of sin. Fudge on our tax forms and we may pay a stiff penalty.
Commit adultery and we risk dissolution of our marriage and alien-
ation from our children. Pad our expense account and we put our jobs
in jeopardy.

For me, here's the encouragement that pulsates from these verses:
Paul put a positive spin on the principle! He sandwiched it between two references to service for the Lord—a call for generosity toward those who
teach God's Word (v. 6) and a plea not to lose heart in doing good (vv.
9–10). He equated "sowing to the Spirit" not only to the financial support
of Christian leaders, but to anything we do for others in Christ's name.
This is tantamount to a promise: *what we sow for the Lord reaps results!*

Viewing from a Long-Range Perspective

The seed metaphor implies that the harvest of our labors is usually not
immediate. There's a good reason *Jack and the Beanstalk* is tagged a fairy
tale: beans don't sprout overnight!

All plant, flower, vegetable, or fruit seeds that achieve growth experience germination. Within each seed is an embryo with the potential of
becoming a visible life form. Germination is the process—often painstakingly slow—during which the sunflower, pumpkin vine, or apple tree
bursts through the shell of the seed, pushes its way through the soil, and

sprouts above ground. How long germination takes varies depending on the type of seed and the condition of the soil, but after sowing, weeks may pass when it appears nothing is happening.

When we sow the seed of God's truth, a type of germination occurs. Since life change is rarely instantaneous, laborers in God's workforce need to think long-term in relation to outcomes. Between sowing and reaping is a time lapse, often lasting years rather than days or weeks. To be realistic, we don't always see a harvest in our lifetime. To stop the lava flow of doubt, we must view Galatians 6:6–10 for what it is: reassurance that "sowing to the Spirit" isn't in vain. For Paul, it was a reason not to lose heart.

What we perceive as a barren time may be a season of sowing that will yet yield a future harvest. Or it may be an incubation period for seeds planted at some point in the past. This seed-sowing metaphor and concept of germination is especially applicable to those of us who teach the Bible in any venue. Seldom does any given lesson or message radically transform a life. Yet the cumulative effect of sowing God's truth over time deepens learners' faith, shapes their values, and instills a more biblical worldview. Just as every seed in a field becomes part of the harvest, every Bible study we lead is an integral part of their spiritual development.

I'm aware that exposure to God's Word doesn't always lead to life change, yet there is no transformation without biblical instruction. R. C. Sproul wrote, "There can be nothing in the heart that is not first in the mind. Though it is possible to have theology in the head without it piercing the soul, it cannot pierce the soul without first being grasped by the mind."[1]

The upshot of this perspective is that we can't accurately gauge the fruitfulness of current endeavors. It's always premature to conclude that nothing of eternal value is happening. If Paul cited the sow-reap principle as a reason not to lose heart in doing good, then we have a reason for optimism when we sow.

An anecdote from church history shows the need to "think in the future tense" about our sowing.

Reaping from a Single Seed

Edward Kimball, whom I introduced in Chapter Nine, reaped what he sowed. More than 150 years later, the repercussions still vibrate the world over.

In 1855, this Boston businessman taught a young men's Sunday school class. An older teen began attending because his uncle, with whom he lived and worked, required church attendance. Kimball realized right away that his newest class member didn't know Christ. The teacher perceived him as spiritually dense, unable to grasp even elementary Bible truths. But Kimball befriended the young man and earned his respect.

Burdened by his class member's spiritual darkness, Kimball visited the uncle's shoe store, presented the plan of salvation, and led the young Dwight L. Moody to faith in Christ. Years later, Moody's evangelistic preaching catapulted him to worldwide renown. In Moody's lifetime, God's grace wooed many thousands to faith through his preaching.

In the late 1870s, Moody exerted a life-changing influence on J. Wilbur Chapman, later a hymn writer and traveling evangelist in his own right. The young Chapman heard Moody preach in Chicago and asked for a personal counseling session afterward. Chapman, plagued by insecurity about a prior conversion experience, confessed uncertainty about his salvation. Moody sowed a seed by showing him John 5:24: "Truly, truly, I say to you, he who hears My word, and believes in Him who sent Me, has eternal life, and does not come into judgment, but has passed out of death into life."

Moody posed a series of questions, probing Chapman's past experience in reference to the content of that Bible verse. Chapman left the session buoyant, absolutely convinced of the efficacy of his conversion. Never again did Chapman doubt his acceptance before God.

Chapman later hired a former pro baseball player, Billy Sunday, to organize Chapman's evangelistic meetings. Chapman's influence spurred Sunday to launch his own evangelistic services across the country. In 1924, a band of businessmen in Charlotte, North Carolina sponsored a successful evangelistic crusade led by Sunday. After those meetings, the sponsors formed the Charlotte Businessman's Club, a group that ten years later invited Mordecai Ham to speak in Charlotte. One of Ham's meetings became a hinge on which the twentieth-century evangelistic movement turned. A young, lanky dairy farmer walked the aisle and surrendered his life to Christ—Billy Graham.

And the story goes on and on! Graham preached to over two billion people in his lifetime. A lady in my church, a diligent volunteer, came to Christ as a child in Graham's 1950 crusade in Columbia, South Carolina.

Back in 1855, Edward Kimball couldn't fathom how his witness to a shoe clerk would alter the landscape of Christianity for generations. Kimball "sowed to the Spirit," and from the gospel seed that he planted, the Holy Spirit still reaps a bountiful harvest.[2]

Sowing to the Spirit

Every time you share your faith with a nonbeliever, you also "sow to the Spirit." Who knows what God will do in and through a person you lead to Christ? You sow to the Spirit each time you pore over a Bible passage for hours before you teach or preach it. Every time you intercede for someone who needs the Lord's intervention. Every time you recruit a committed member to teach God's Word to kids in Sunday school. Every time you write a letter to a despondent friend and include the Bible verses that once injected hope in your own lethargic spirit. Every time . . .

You get the idea. The next time you doubt if God will do anything with the seeds you plant, remember the yield it produced through a single seed sown by a Sunday school teacher named Edward Kimball.

Dig Deeper

Examine Acts 16:14, a reference to Lydia's conversion in Philippi.

What is significant about these words: "The Lord opened her heart to respond to the things spoken by Paul"?

How does this statement correlate with the concept of "sowing and reaping?"

External factors affect the germination of seeds: water, temperature, oxygen, and sometimes the amount of light. Similarly, when we "sow to the Spirit" through teaching and evangelism, certain factors will either expedite or hinder the process of germination. One variable that facilitates the germination process is prayer for the seeds we've sown to take root and produce fruit. Our prayers for effectiveness and for those we serve have the same effect as a lingering shower to a recently-sown garden. Our praying acknowledges the Holy Spirit's role in the germination process. Successful sowing is never merely a human endeavor.

CHAPTER 18

The Pressure Is Off

Picture yourself as a parent of a college girl who has two dilemmas common among students: low grades and no money. She needs to break this news to you, but she figures you'll blow your top and have trouble understanding. What strategy will she employ?

Charles Swindoll tells about a coed in precisely this situation. She used a creative approach to soften the blows of reality. Here's the letter to her parents written prior to the proliferation of e-mails. Swindoll's comments follow her letter:

"Dear Mom and Dad,

"Just thought I'd drop you a note to clue you in on my plans. I've fallen in love with a guy named Jim. He quit high school after grade eleven to get married. About a year ago he got a divorce.

"We've been going steady for two months and plan to get married in the fall. Until then, I've decided to move into his apartment (I think I might be pregnant).

"At any rate, I dropped out of school last week, although I'd like to finish college sometime in the future."

On the next page of the letter, she continued:

"Mom and Dad, I just want you to know that everything I've written so far in this letter is false. NONE of it is true.

"But Mom and Dad, it IS true that I got a C in French and flunked Math. It IS true that I'm going to need some more money for my tuition payments."

Pretty sharp coed! Even bad news can sound like good news if it is seen from a certain vantage point. So much in life depends on "where you're coming from" as you face your circumstances. The secret, of course, is perspective.[1]

Perspective is as advantageous to Christian workers as it was for the coed. Perspective is the capacity to view things in their true relations or relative importance. It's the ability to see clearly in light of a bigger picture, to view things more accurately in light of our limited understanding. The coed knew that poor grades and an empty pocketbook were minor matters compared to the fictional circumstances on page one of her letter.

Biblical perspective is especially vital when we don't seem to be bearing fruit. When it comes to the lack of observable results in ministry, we need God's viewpoint before we start classifying ourselves as incompetent, failures, or lacking in consecration.

Who's Responsible?

A theological perspective that bolsters me during a ministry drought is this: *fruit is ultimately God's responsibility, not mine.* When I mine God's Word, I find the following nuggets in its rich soil. When I can't see results, I preach to myself these verses and stories.

Acts 16:13–14. On Paul's second missionary trip, the Holy Spirit commandeered his travel itinerary and directed his team to Philippi. When Paul explained the gospel of Jesus Christ to Lydia, "*The Lord opened her heart* to respond to the things spoken by Paul" (emphasis mine).

Though God's Spirit employed a human agent to communicate the gospel, Lydia didn't owe her conversion merely to Paul's proclamation. Bearing fruit in evangelism required divine intervention in the form of making Lydia's heart receptive. This text beams a bright spotlight on God's sovereign role in ministry success.

First Corinthians 3:1–9. Believers in Corinth rallied around human leaders rather than Christ himself. Paul initially shared the gospel with them, followed by Apollos' fruitful labor among them. Divisions surfaced based on which leader folks aligned themselves with. Neither Paul nor Apollos encouraged this "party spirit."

To diffuse the tension, Paul minimized the role of human agents and magnified the work of God among the Corinthians: "What then is Apollos? And what is Paul? Servants through whom you believed, even as the Lord gave *opportunity* to each one. I planted, Apollos watered, *but God was causing the growth*. So then neither the one who plants nor the one who waters is anything, but *God who causes the growth*" (vv. 5–7, emphasis mine). God assumed responsibility for fruitfulness in Corinth, just as he did in Philippi.

First Corinthians 12:4–6. Within his longest discourse on spiritual gifts, Paul says there are "varieties of gifts" distributed by the Holy Spirit. He gives different gifts to different individuals. There are "varieties of ministries," or diverse venues, where we exercise our gifts, governed by the Lord Jesus Christ (v. 5). And he refers to "varieties of effects" superintended by "the same God who works all things in all *persons*" (v. 6). Verse six indicates that God himself supplies the power and energizes the gifts so they produce an effect on people.

Jeremiah and Jonah. That outcomes hinge more on God's sovereignty than on his servants is seen most vividly in the contrast between these prophets. Jeremiah complied with God's initial call and served for four decades with little to show for it. Jonah's initial response to God's call was to hop a ship going in the opposite direction. When Jonah relented and preached in Nineveh, he rued the Ninevites' repentance and God's cancellation of the city's destruction.

Why did the reluctant, disloyal prophet bear more fruit than the obedient one? The answer remains a mystery. We can't explain one's success and the other's drought by the quality of their character or the skill of their performances. Similarly, your barrenness and another's fruitfulness doesn't necessarily mean God favors you less or that you're doing something wrong.

Bearing versus *Producing* Fruit

In John 15:1–6, eight times Jesus refers to our fruitbearing. This call to bear fruit includes productive ministry as well as cultivation of positive character. But paradoxically, *he calls us to bear fruit that only he can produce.* "I am the vine, you are the branches; he who abides in Me and I in Him, he bears much fruit; for apart from Me you can do nothing" (v. 5).

We may *bear* the fruit, but only the vine *produces* it. What are the implications of this insight? Awareness that God, not us, produces the fruit should prompt us to "abide in the vine" (v. 4), which is a prerequisite for fruitfulness. Maintaining intimacy with the Lord is our only responsibility. Without such intimacy, Oswald Chambers believed we're prone to worship God's work more than him: "Beware of any work which enables you to evade concentration on Him . . . the only responsibility you have is to keep in living constant touch with God."[2]

Also, knowing that our ministry isn't merely a human endeavor, but an effort requiring God's penetration of others' hearts, should spur us to pray more for persons we serve. Perhaps we're never more fruitful than when we admit our limitations and appeal to God for results.

Who's in Charge?

The last word on God's responsibility for results in our ministry is Psalm 103:19: "The LORD has established His throne in the heavens, and His sovereignty rules over all." For David Cashin, professor of Intercultural Studies at Columbia International University, God's sovereignty is an encouraging perspective, not a sterile doctrine. He views his years of missionary service in Bangladesh through the lens of these words:

> Americans think that if we follow our systems and methods correctly, we'll achieve what we want. This makes it all depend on us. When the system fails, we think that God is somehow dependent on us and if we cannot do it then it can't be done. That makes God no bigger than we are. This is the most important lesson I ever learned as a missionary: it does not depend on me, and God is sovereign in all He does.[3]

If success depends more on God than us, if he's ultimately responsible for outcomes, then on what basis does he evaluate his servants? What keeps this perspective on God's sovereignty from degenerating into an unhealthy fatalism and a lackadaisical attitude? If these questions percolate in your mind, consult the next chapter.

═══ Dig Deeper ═══

Review these Bible passages cited in this chapter: Acts 16:13–14; 1 Corinthians 3:1–9; 1 Corinthians 12:4–6, and John 15:1–6. Then mull over these questions:

How do these passages explain the chapter title "The Pressure Is Off"?

Which Bible passage makes the strongest case for the truth of this chapter: *fruit is ultimately God's responsibility, not ours?*

Though God's sovereignty determines outcomes, he nonetheless works through human agents. Ministry is a cooperative effort between

God and us. To succeed, we need the Holy Spirit's intervention. What are some applications of this truth?

CHAPTER 19

LIBERATION FROM THE SUCCESS SYNDROME

HERE'S A HILARIOUS STORY DISHED UP BY CHARLES SWINDOLL:

A friend of mine ate dog food one evening. No, he wasn't actually at a fraternity initiation or a hobo party . . . he was actually at an elegant student reception in a physician's home near Miami. The dog food was served on delicate little crackers with a wedge of imported cheese, bacon chips, an olive, and a sliver of pimento on top. That's right, friends and neighbors, it was hors d'oeuvres á la Alpo.

The hostess is a first-class nut! You gotta know her to appreciate the story. She had just graduated from a gourmet cooking course, and so she decided it was time to put her skill to the ultimate test. Did she ever! After doctoring up those miserable morsels and putting them on a couple of silver trays, with a sly grin she watched them disappear. One guy (my friend) couldn't get enough. He kept coming back for more. I don't recall how they broke the news to him . . . but when he found out the truth, he probably barked and bit her leg! He certainly must have gagged a little.[1]

That's a classic example of deception! The hostess tricked her guests into thinking they were eating expensive snack food concocted in her upper-class kitchen. Instead, she made her pet cocker spaniel howling mad by giving away his supper.

In his efforts to derail persons in ministry, Satan expertly disguises the truth concerning what constitutes success. Here's the morsel he wants us to swallow: *success in serving God is gauged by results. If you're not bearing obvious fruit, you're a failure.*

If we pick from Satan's platter and digest his perspective about ministry, doubts about our calling and giftedness will at some point smother initiative and cause passion to leak. The sobering truth is that *we can't guarantee results, particularly when it comes to folks' responsiveness to God.* Neither giftedness nor diligence guarantees the outcome we're after.

If you're ready to throw in the towel over anemic results, remember the principle of the previous chapter: *fruitfulness is ultimately God's responsibility, not yours.* Varying results among his workers aren't necessarily explained by their levels of consecration or degrees of effort.

This chapter offers another reassuring slant on success. In tandem with awareness of God's sovereignty, what you read in subsequent paragraphs should alleviate feelings of inferiority or inadequacy stemming from unfavorable comparison to others' ministries. And you'll discover what God esteems more than external indicators of success. *It's something you can control, and digesting this concept won't cause indigestion!*

Personal Profiles

Jeremiah prophesied in the southern kingdom of Judah during the last forty years of its existence, prior to the deportation of God's people to Babylonia. He observed the moral disintegration of the nation and the devastating consequences of God's discipline. Folks did not heed Jeremiah's forecasts of God's judgment nor his call for repentance.

With little to show for his preaching, you can sense his frustration in these words: "I have spoken to you again and again, but you have not listened" (Jer. 25:3). Their resistance and God's impending judgment broke his heart. "I weep; my eyes run down with water" (Lam. 1:16). His audience ridiculed and persecuted him.

God gave Ezekiel a similar message of repentance, but his call came with disheartening news: "The house of Israel is not willing to listen to you," said the Lord, "since they are not willing to listen to me" (Ezek. 3:7). God predicted a lack of success, yet insisted that Ezekiel follow through and convey his words to them: "Speak to them and tell them, whether they listen or not, 'thus says the LORD God'" (v. 11). If he didn't warn them, Ezekiel would be held responsible for the blood of the wicked. If Ezekiel relayed God's message, he would deliver himself (vv. 11–21). God held Ezekiel accountable for communicating the message, not for Israel's response to it.

Turn left in your Bible, back to the time of Moses' leadership during the wilderness wanderings of God's people. When folks complained vociferously about a lack of water, God told Moses, "Speak to the rock before their eyes, that it may yield its water" (Num. 20:8). Moses said to the people, "You rebels, shall we bring forth water for you out of this rock?" (v. 10). Next, instead of speaking to the rock as God had instructed, Moses whacked it with his rod.

On a previous occasion, God provided water for the people by telling Moses to strike a rock. But this time, hitting the rock defied God's commands. Striking the stone also demonstrated Moses' lack of trust. Would merely speaking to it this time get the job done? On top of that, Moses' pride surfaced. He considered himself a partner with God in doing the miraculous, for he said, "shall *we* bring forth water?" (emphasis mine).

Based solely on external results, Moses' leadership on this occasion was wildly successful. Water gushed out, quenching the thirst of the multitudes. Yet God wasn't happy, accusing Moses of unbelief and failing to treat him as holy in the eyes of the Israelites. As a consequence, God informed Moses that he'd never set foot in the Promised Land of Canaan.

Contrast the stories of Jeremiah and Ezekiel with Moses' behavior. The prophets carried out their calling with little to show for it. Despite his disobedience, unbelief, and pride, Moses got results.

In addition to the truth of God's sovereignty, what can we glean from these profiles concerning God's view of success?

Redefining Success

Because folks disregarded their message, the prophets were no less commendable to God. Their predicament, coupled with the contrast between Moses' results and God's displeasure toward him, suggests that *God evaluates his servants on the basis of faithfulness to his call, not fruitfulness*. Normally faithfulness to a task spawns effectiveness, but Jeremiah and Ezekiel were notable exceptions.

This insight encourages me because faithfulness is a factor I can control! Charles Colson, the late prolific author and founder of Prison Fellowship, once said, "God's call is to be faithful rather than successful. We must continually use the measure of our obedience to the guidelines of His Word as the real—and only—standard of our 'success,' not some more supposedly tangible or glamorous scale."[2]

You can prepare meticulously for the Bible study you lead or the sermon you deliver, but you can't guarantee a teachable spirit or change of heart among persons who attend.

Share your faith winsomely with your neighbors, yet they may still rebuff Christ.

Implement all the volunteer recruitment tips covered in your seminary course on church leadership, but many members will still snub your invitation to teach Sunday school.

Work harder at raising money for your parachurch organization or Christian school, but your fundraising might still come up short of the budget.

You're a conduit through whom God's Spirit flows, but your responsibility ends with obedience to your God-called task.

Period.

Success Story

A missionary couple, having completed their first four-year term in a Muslim country, lamented the lack of results. Accompanying the lack of conversions to Christ had been sick children, social ostracism by members of the community, and harassment from gangs of kids who pelted their tin roof with rocks throughout the night.

During a stateside interview, a missionary executive figured they wanted to start all over in a different location within the same country. While citing several options for their relocation, the couple interrupted him, expressing a willingness to return to the same place.

With disbelief, the executive said, "In spite of all you've encountered, the difficulties your family would face with no assurance of results, you'd be willing to spend another four years in this situation?"

"Yes," they assured him. The young husband and father continued: "When we arrived there after language school and realized what we were up against, we reconciled ourselves to the fact that God had not called us to personal fulfillment or success, but to obedience. If this is where God wants us, we won't consider anywhere else."[3]

Despite their dismay, this missionary couple was more successful than they thought.

Words of Qualification

First, hold this "success is faithfulness, not results" principle in tension with the point of Chapter Seventeen, "Reaping What You Sow." There, I reassured you with verses promising a harvest from your efforts.

View these two perspectives as complementary, not contradictory. You won't always see the desired outcomes from a particular event, encounter, or message. Yet God's Word does promise that over time, your efforts won't be in vain.

Jeremiah and Ezekiel's words, preserved for future generations of God's people, eventually exerted a positive impact. After the severe discipline of captivity and the subsequent restoration of a remnant, what the prophets had written became more valuable to God's people. Their warnings about the consequences of sin, coupled with their reminders of God's faithfulness, found a more receptive audience. What Jeremiah and Ezekiel said as God's spokesmen still informs us more than twenty-five hundred years later! In their books, they speak to us about God's heart for holiness, the painful consequences of sin, and God's grace in forgiving sinners.

Also, *defining success as faithfulness instead of results doesn't excuse mediocrity*. Faithfulness demands diligence, evaluations of our ministry, and ongoing training to hone our skills.

Robertson McQuilkin, missionary statesman and former President of Columbia International University, says, "The emphasis on faithfulness shouldn't preclude self-examination when we aren't seeing fruit. If a ministry that was once effective is now barren, I suggest asking ourselves these questions: Am I still connected to the Vine (John 15:4)? Am I praying less about my tasks? Am I compromising morally?"[4]

Regarding a venture that has never yielded fruit, McQuilkin added these questions: "Am I certain God called me to it? Am I gifted for this responsibility? Should I try to teach a different age level or select a different sphere of service altogether?"

Neither a poor fit or moral compromises or prayerlessness may explain a lack of results, but I'd be remiss if I didn't include his questions.

If your branches appear bare, your walk with God is intact, and you're diligent in your ministry, preach to yourself these complementary perspectives: *Ultimately, God is responsible for results. I succeed in his eyes when I'm faithful to what he asks me to do.*

Dig Deeper

Read chapters 2 and 3 of Ezekiel. What did God consider "success" for Ezekiel?

In relation to your current sphere of service, ask God's Spirit to reveal answers to these questions: What would faithfulness to your calling look like? Do you need to make any changes before you will be able to hear these words from God: "Well done, good and faithful servant"?

CHAPTER 20

PROMISE KEEPER

"IF I'M HIRED, I'LL STAY ON STAFF AT LEAST THREE YEARS."

That's the assurance a youth ministry candidate gave the senior pastor. Twelve months after he accepted the position, the young man left for a prime teaching position in a Christian school at a beach resort.

———

A prosperous businessman heard a stirring presentation in his church by a prospective missionary couple. After the service, he told them he would personally send $200 a month toward their support. Neither the couple nor their mission agency ever heard from him.

———

When a winsome couple responded with an enthusiastic "yes!," the children's pastor thanked the Lord for filling the first-grade Sunday school opening. A week later, they backed out, citing the number of weekends they travel.

———

When folks break their promises, disillusionment envelopes us. But we all know a few folks whose word we can bank on: those who don't divulge the personal information we share. Those who follow through with their pledge to return our phone call or text message. Those who spurn an opportunity to have an affair due to the vow they made at the altar. Those who keep a commitment no matter how much it inconveniences them. Those persons pass the test posed by Psalm 15:4, which insists that a person of integrity "swears to his own hurt and does not change."

A long time ago I became convinced that *a promise is only as good as the person who makes it*. That's why I take the promises in God's Word seriously: they're firmly fastened to his character!

Paul insisted that God "cannot lie" (Tit. 1:2). In contrast to our inconsistency, "He remains faithful; for He cannot deny himself" (2 Tim. 2:13). In reference to God's against-all-odds pledge of an heir, Abraham was "fully assured that what God had promised, He was able also to perform" (Rom. 4:21). And no passage makes this point more vividly than Numbers 23:19: "God is not a man, that He should lie, nor a son of man, that He should repent; Has He said, and will He not do it? Or has He spoken, and will He not make it good?"

Sermon Preparation

God's Word salutes the value of knowing its own promises. According to 2 Peter 1:4, hiding them in our hearts promotes holiness: "He has granted to us His precious and magnificent promises, so that by them you might become partakers of *the* divine nature, having escaped the corruption that is in the world by lust."

Another reason to familiarize ourselves with God's promises is the soul-sustenance they provide for those of us involved in his work. Back in the Introduction of this book, I explained the concept of "preaching to yourself"—giving biblically-informed rebuttals to negative thinking, or combating everything from discouragement to temptation with the truths of God's Word. Memorizing selected Bible verses provides the raw material necessary for this biblical form of self-talk and nudges me closer to God-centered rather than self-centered thinking.

In the remainder of this chapter, I'll set my scope on seven promises I preach to myself when my passion for ministry wanes or discouragement threatens my perseverance. Without a flicker of hesitation, I can say that my memorization of these verses supplies biblical anchors that keep me afloat.

Eternal Dividends

Church members faced persecution from unbelievers. Factions within the church, plus the fallout from one member's hideous sexual sin, threatened the congregation's spiritual vitality. Paul didn't want these factors to squash their enthusiasm for Christ, nor squelch their witness in the community. To instill persistence in the work of the church, God provided this promise to the Corinthians—and to us—through Paul's pen: "Therefore, my beloved brethren, be steadfast, immovable, always abounding in the work of the Lord, knowing that your toil is not *in* vain in the Lord" (1 Cor. 15:58).

How does this verse inform our spheres of service?

1. *Sticking to the ministry he's given will eventually yield eternal dividends.* The term "not in vain" means "not empty or worthless; not void of substance or content." Whether or not we see the fruit, God assures us our labor isn't wasted.

2. *Our ministries belong to God and he's responsible to empower us for what he assigns us.* What we do is the "work *of the Lord*" and it's "not in vain *in the Lord*." Results don't hinge so much on our giftedness or diligence as on *his* competence and faithfulness.

3. *Positive outcomes from our labor are as certain as Jesus' resurrection.* The "therefore" at the start of verse 58 alludes to the content of verses 1–57, where Paul cites evidences of Jesus' resurrection and discusses the nature of our own resurrected bodies. If the gospel isn't a hoax and Jesus didn't stay dead, then what we do for him counts!

I played back my mental tape of 1 Corinthians 15:58 when a student where I teach slandered me by spreading a false rumor, when unremitting back pain hindered my concentration as I studied and taught, when I discovered that my retirement account paled in comparison to that of a friend who teaches at a state university, when acquisition editors kept passing on a book idea that I knew God had inspired.

The context and content of verse 58 reminds me that immortality is laboring at an eternal task. Preaching 1 Corinthians 15:58 to yourself could become the most faith-boosting sermon you'll ever hear.

A Promised Place

Set your scope on Jesus' words in John 14:1–3:

> Do not let your heart be troubled; believe in God, believe also in Me. In My Father's house are many dwelling places; if it were not so, I would have told you; for I go to prepare a place for you. If I go and prepare a place for you, I will come again and receive you to Myself, that where I am, there you may be also.

Leadership books extol working with a "big picture in mind" and "thinking in the future tense." Focusing on a desired outcome engenders perseverance, enabling the leader to overcome obstacles and trudge through uninspired moments.

Similarly, the bedrock premise of heaven unveils our ultimate destination, and that of people won to Christ through our labor. Why we work so hard crystallizes. We realize that there's a date after which foes won't badger us. We're energized, knowing that someday heaven is where we'll get our mail.

Of special significance is the emphatic nature of Jesus' words. He didn't merely announce that a construction crew was working on our dwelling place. Jesus added an exclamation point to the promise when he said, "If it were not so, I would have told you."

If Jesus emphasized it, I believe it.

*For additional coverage of the value of an eternal perspective, see Chapter Twenty-Three, "Don't Lose Heart."

Divine Discernment

Responsibility for decision making fosters stress. What we choose impacts others. Which youth ministry candidate to hire; which strategic initiative to adopt; where to make the bloodletting cuts in the proposed budget; what to say to the troubled soul who comes to you in a last-ditch effort to find hope—the answers to such dilemmas usually aren't clear-cut. That's when we retrieve the following verses from our database.

"I will instruct you and teach you in the way which you should go; I will counsel you with My eye upon you" (Ps. 32:8).

"But if any of you lacks wisdom, let him ask of God, who gives to all men generously and without reproach, and it will be given to him" (James 1:5).

The smartest choice we can make is to acknowledge our lack of wisdom before God and to plead with him for discernment. Then we trust him to nudge us in the right direction, because he said he would. Our confidence isn't in our discernment so much as it is in his Word.

James 1:5 comes on the heels of a section dealing with trials (vv. 2–4). James cites the inevitability of adversity and explains its character-enhancing potential. In this context, wisdom is the capacity to respond and to choose appropriately when the heat is on high.

What trial stemming from your ministry requires divine insight to handle? Will you take God at his Word and expect him to show you the wisest alternative?

Seniors with Savvy

Sometimes the effects of aging cool off passion and lower confidence for serving the Lord. Pain racks our bodies, threatening ineffectiveness. Energy wanes, limiting output.

Even if we need hearing aids to decipher it, God has a word for seniors: "You who have been borne by Me from birth and have been carried from the womb; even to *your* old age, I will be the same, and even to *your* graying years I will bear *you*! I have done *it*, and I will carry *you*, and I will hear *you* and I will deliver *you*" (Isa. 46:3–4).

Just as God expected the people of Israel to keep their eyes locked on him and not on their own frailty, he wants us to rely on his strength as our own declines. No matter how wrinkled or weak we get, as long as he keeps us around, he'll empower us for what he calls us to do. In the same chapter of Isaiah, God assured them, "My purpose will be established, And I will accomplish all My good pleasure" (v. 10).

A reason to trust his promise of support in our later years is his past faithfulness. The One who assures us that he'll "bear" us, "carry" us, and "deliver" us during graying years is the One who has sustained us from the womb.

Isaiah 46:3–4 works in tandem with Psalm 92:14, where the writer compares the righteous to a flourishing plant: "They will still yield fruit in old age; They shall be full of sap and very green."

Nobody outlives the promises of God.

An Inside Job

When Bible truths I communicate seemingly go in one ear of listeners and out the other . . .

When weariness from work assaults my spirit, leaving a pock-marked resolve . . .

When hecklers in the form of doubts crack my brittle confidence . . .

When Satan's lies start sounding sensible and skew my perspective on sacrifice . . .

Then I frame these words and hang them prominently on the wall of my mind: "For it is God who is at work in you, both to will and to work for *His* good pleasure" (Phil. 2:13).

I tap into a resource far exceeding my own gifts and experience. (*God is at work.*) I don't have to conjure up pep rally enthusiasm for a project. (*He instills the will or resolve within me.*) The most desirable outcome isn't a particular goal I set or my personal satisfaction. (*What matters is his good pleasure.*)

Countless times, I've brandished the sword of Philippians 2:13 in the fight against discouragement.

Weapon of Warfare

Venture into service for the Lord and a hungry beast stalks us: "Be of sober *spirit*, be on the alert. Your adversary, the devil, prowls about like a roaring lion, seeking someone to devour" (1 Pet. 5:8). Opposition may escalate. Temptations we thought we had outgrown rejuvenate, increasing our vulnerability to sin. If the Son of God waged warfare using Scripture (see Matt. 4:1–11), we must wield this weapon as well.

I often make a desperate jab at the enemy with 2 Thessalonians 3:3: "But the Lord is faithful, and He will strengthen and protect you from the evil *one*." What prompted Paul to write this promise was his request for prayer, "that the word of the Lord will spread rapidly and be glorified" (v. 1). But with the same stroke of his pen, he acknowledged that "perverse and evil men" oppose the spread of the gospel (v. 2).

No matter how strong the lure is, our yielding to temptation isn't inevitable. This promise reminds us of the reassuring words a prophet delivered when God's people were paralyzed with fear, cowering at the thought of armies from multiple countries invading Judah: "Do not fear or be dismayed because of this great multitude, for the battle is not yours, but God's" (2 Chron. 20:15).

When it comes to warfare, God is still undefeated.

---

*For an encouraging perspective on spiritual warfare against God's servants, see Chapter Seven, "Rousing The Enemy."

Affluent Father

Be honest now. Do you ever envy persons who live more comfortably, who never run out of money before they run out of month? Do unpaid bills ignite worry?

If your move to the mission field is on hold due to anemic financial support, do you handle it with aplomb, or does frustration birth doubts about God's call?

Does the graph revealing giving patterns to your church or organization slope downward, agitating you because you can't launch new ministry initiatives?

A promise that allays my personal anxieties about money is Philippians 4:19: "My God shall supply all your needs according to His riches in glory in Christ Jesus."

Here are penetrating questions the Holy Spirit asks me concerning this verse: Paul penned this promise to church members who gave sacrificially to support his itinerant ministry. Why is this context significant? If I'm short of anticipated funds, could it mean that God wants to address a need in my life far more pressing than the material one? Or does it suggest that God's perception of what constitutes a "need" differs from mine? Is he trying to wean me from circumstances as the basis of my contentment? (According to Phil. 4:11, Paul had learned to be content no matter what the circumstances.) What needs outside the scope of finances does this pledge address?

Knowing I have a well-to-do Father who loves me goes a long way to assuage anxiety.

God's love prompts him to stock his Word with hope-galvanizing promises. His power enables him to keep his word.

Dig Deeper

Which promise cited in this chapter resonates most with you right now? Why?

To foil despondency about your ministry, or to buttress sagging motivation, memorize 1 Corinthians 15:58 this week.

In *The Spirit of the Disciplines*, Dallas Willard accentuates the necessity of Scripture memory for an individual and a church. Though he doesn't mention God's promises specifically, perhaps the choicest verses to hide in your heart are God's promises to his people.

> As a pastor, teacher, and counselor, I have repeatedly seen the transformation of inner and outer life that comes simply from memorization and meditation upon Scripture. Personally, I would never undertake to pastor a church or guide a program of Christian education that did not involve a continuous program of memorization of the choicest passages of Scripture for people of all ages.
>
> . . . [We] *meditate* on what comes before us; that is, we withdraw into silence where we prayerfully and steadily focus upon it. In this way its meaning for us can emerge and form us as God works in the depths of our heart, mind, and soul. We devote long periods of time to this. Our prayer as we study meditatively is always that God would meet with us and speak specifically to us, for ultimately the Word of God is God speaking.[1]

CHAPTER 21

DELAYS ARE NOT DENIALS

The Discipline of Delay, Part 1

HAVE YOU EVER BEEN IN A HURRY, BUT GOD WASN'T?

Brad and Susan's return to the mission field has been delayed two years due to inadequate financial support. They're chomping at the bit to fulfill their call to plant churches in Mexico.

Joe, a pastor, has labored long and hard, yearning for a fresh moving of God's Spirit within his congregation. But after six years, instead of revival, he sees bickering and lethargy.

Since Andy finished seminary six months ago, he has sent his résumé to a number of churches without garnering a job offer.

Hope flickers within Ron, a seminary professor, whose fifteen-year stretch of intercession for a spiritually-wayward adult daughter hasn't made any apparent difference.

———————— ⇒ ————————

For over two years, First Church has looked for a new pastor. Despite search committee members meeting twice a month, and occasionally traveling on weekends, few prospective candidates have expressed interest. And a couple of church families, disgruntled over a lack of leadership, recently left.

———————— ⇒ ————————

When we encounter gut-wrenching delays, the waiting seems absurd, a waste of time.

Nothing challenges my own faith more than waiting. That's why I delved into a study of this theme in Scripture, examining the lives of saints who waited on God for a long time. As I pored over their stories, reasons for delay crystallized and I saw what God wants his servants to do while they wait. What I learned doesn't make waiting a rollicking good time for me, but it does temper my inherent impatience with helpful biblical perspectives.

Nobody waited longer on God than Abraham.

Twenty-Five-Year Hiatus

When God first promised him an heir, Abraham was seventy-five years old and Sarah a decade younger. Given their age, you'd think God wouldn't wait long to open her womb. Yet eleven years passed without any morning sickness. Then, thinking God may intend to circumvent his wife to produce an heir, he agreed with Sarah's idea of fathering a child with Hagar, her maid. But Ishmael wasn't God's choice of a covenant child. When Abraham reached one hundred and Sarah ninety, she delivered Isaac.

Familiarity with the story makes it easy to gloss over what was likely going on inside Abraham. How would we handle a twenty-five-year span between the promise of an heir and his birth? As their wrinkles deepened and the likelihood of their impotence increased, what feelings gnawed at his confidence that Sarah would bear him a child? What thoughts rattled around inside his head?

Despite his subsequent liaison with Hagar, trust marked Abraham's initial response to God's promise: "He believed in the LORD, and He reckoned it to him as righteousness" (Gen. 15:6). But we'd be naïve not to think that the ensuing delay sorely tested his faith in God's character. He probably vacillated between confidence and doubt. Troubling questions likely surfaced: *Will God keep his Word? Can he do what's humanly impossible in Sarah's womb?*

Perhaps every year he waited chipped away at his confidence that God would follow through. It's one thing to regurgitate God's attributes on a theology quiz; it's another thing altogether when frustrating life experiences pose the exam questions.

Ironically, the delay that tested Abraham's faith also solidified it. The process of questioning God, of facing an uncertain outcome, forced Abraham to pour out his feelings to God, to meditate on past instances of God's faithfulness, to conclude that the object of his faith was dependable even when the amount of his faith was scant. In the crucible of inner conflict, he discovered the veracity of Ron Dunn's words: "A man will never trust God until *he has to.*"[1] Though he couldn't claim undiluted trust, Abraham's faith endured. He never stopped building altars and calling on God. Generations later, James—himself a product of God's promise to the father of the Jewish nation—cited a benefit of trials that Abraham learned through the discipline of delay: "The testing of your faith produces endurance. And let endurance have *its* perfect result, that you may be perfect and complete, lacking in nothing" (James 1:3–4).

"Testing" carries the idea of *proving* or *authenticating*. The term described the process of trying out mineral ore to determine the amount and quality of gold it contained with the goal of preparing and approving it for use.

A few years after Isaac's birth, we see the kind of faith in Abraham that had been forged in the furnace of waiting. God challenged his trust in even more dramatic fashion, instructing him to sacrifice Isaac as a burnt offering. God had announced that through this heir, Abraham's descendants would rival the number of stars in the sky (Gen. 15:4–5). God's strange command seemed incompatible with the promise.

Like a rope that's stronger when its hemps are twisted and stretched, twenty-five years of waiting on God had strengthened Abraham's capacity to trust him. And Isaac's birth had vindicated Abraham's faith. Though he couldn't wrap his mind around God's command to sacrifice Isaac, there's evidence he nonetheless exhibited rock-ribbed faith in God's previous promise of descendants. *He expected Isaac to survive or figured God would resurrect him!* Before ascending the mountain where he'd offer the sacrifice, Abraham told his servants, "*We* will worship and return to you" (Gen. 22:5, emphasis mine). The delay that had tested his faith also proved its quality, resulting in a thumbs up from God.

When I come to Abraham's story in my annual trek through the Bible, God's Spirit whispers to me: *Sometimes waiting is My will. My delays are never my denials.* Faith pleases God (Heb. 11:6), so it's only logical for him to act in ways that deepen it.

From Prominence to Prison

You've probably heard Joseph's story since you were in kindergarten. Sold to Ishmaelite traders by jealous brothers, the captain of Pharaoh's palace guard obtained him. Potiphar recognized Joseph's leadership skills and God's blessing of his endeavors. He delegated to Joseph his business deals and management of his possessions.

Next came the attempted seduction by Potiphar's wife, Joseph's adamant refusal, and her unjust accusation that landed him in jail for over two years.

We know the rest of the story. How Pharaoh rewarded Joseph for interpreting his dreams. Joseph's management of crop storage during seven years of plenty to prepare for seven subsequent years of devastating famine. Egypt's survival, as well as that of Joseph's family in nearby Canaan, depended on his wise supervision of the nationwide harvesting program. But when Potiphar tossed him into jail, Joseph didn't have the script for his life that revealed a brighter future. He didn't know when or if he'd get out. A shroud of uncertainty covered him and his innocence didn't seem to matter.

The Genesis narrative insists that God was "with Joseph" during his incarceration, just as he had been during the time Joseph served Potiphar (Gen. 39:23). If God hadn't abandoned him, why did he allow Joseph to languish in prison? How could the delay possibly benefit Joseph or expedite God's purpose for his life? Or were the two years wasted—an unnecessary detour to God's plan?

Though resisting the lure of Potiphar's wife demonstrated strong moral fiber, Joseph's character wasn't flawless. As a teen, he dreamed that his brothers' bundles of grain bowed low before his bundle. He didn't wait long to tell them his dream, fueling their anger and taunting.

Despite their negative reaction, he didn't hesitate to describe his next dream to them, either: the sun, moon, and eleven stars bowed down to him. Joseph didn't know precisely what God had in store for him, yet the dreams forecasted some sort of prominence. Was he flaunting his perceived favor in front of his brothers? Did pride prompt the pronouncement of his dreams?

I can't answer in the affirmative for certain, but there is a hint of his need for additional character development in Psalm 105:16-19. These verses reveal a divine rationale for Joseph's imprisonment:

> He called for a famine upon the land;
> . . . He sent a man before them,
> Joseph, *who* was sold as a slave.

> They afflicted his feet with fetters,
> He himself was laid in irons;
> Until the time that his word came to pass,
> *The word of the* LORD *tested him.* (Final emphasis mine.)

Here the term "tested" means "refined." Similar to the Greek term in James 1:3, it referred to the process of removing coarse elements of mineral ore in order to purify and to prepare for usefulness.

Job referred to this same God-initiated refining process: "But He knows the way I take; When He has tried me, I shall come forth as gold" (Job 23:10). The goldsmith hovered over the crucible in which he heated raw ore. As he increased the intensity of the fire, the ore began to melt. He persisted in blowing on the draft until the seething, tortured mass began to separate. The heavy metal settled in the bottom of the crucible; the lighter slag floated to the top. With a ladle, he skimmed off the slag and discarded it, keeping the heat high until the gold was completely melted and was reduced to a growing liquid. When the liquid gold became so clear that he could see his face mirrored in it, he extinguished the fire. The gold was ready for use.

Merrill Tenney had the goldsmith's routine in mind when he wrote: "Sometimes God puts his servants in the crucible. The fire of adversity is hot, and our best intentions evaporate. . . . God is simply trying out the gold to remove the slag. When He can see his face in us, He will put out the fire."[2]

Psalm 105:16–19 suggests that God employed Joseph's delay to remove slag from his character. God wanted to see his reflection in Joseph. Charles Spurgeon linked these verses to Joseph's time in prison, concluding: "Delayed blessing tests people, and proves the metal, whether their faith is of that precious kind which can endure the fire."[3]

The psalmist's commentary on Joseph helps me interpret a disappointing experience of my own.

Slag Removal

In my mid-twenties, on the heels of earning a graduate degree in communications, a well-known evangelical leader recruited me for a new publishing venture. He wanted me to help write innovative, family-based church curriculum and accompany him on the seminar circuit to train teachers who utilized the materials. I relished the chance to work alongside this prolific figure, but six months after moving across the country to start work, my grandiose ministry dreams evaporated. The outside funding for his renewal organization dried up. About the time I received my final paycheck, my wife became pregnant. She couldn't maintain a job due to extreme fatigue and morning sickness. I scrounged for freelance writing jobs. Depression darkened my spirit.

During those difficult months, I vented my disappointment to God and prayed more than usual. God's Spirit used the setback to expose a proud spirit, showing me that a wrong motive had coaxed me into taking the position. I was enamored by the privilege of working with a renowned author and church consultant. My goal—to achieve name recognition like him—eclipsed a desire to serve and honor the Lord. Tears of brokenness and confession soon replaced my weeping over unfulfilled aspirations. Not only did God's Spirit purify my motives, he also used this disillusionment to call me back to Wheaton, Illinois, for a second master's degree in Christian education. That degree launched a new venture in church and higher education that has lasted almost four decades.

Now you know why V. Raymond Edman's remarks on delay resonate with me. His words describe what happened to Joseph as well.

> Have you come to the discipline of delay? Inactivity you have for activity, weakness for strength, silence for speaking, . . . obscurity for opportunity? Let the darkness of delay discipline your soul in the patience of the saints, in the promises of God. . . . *Delay never thwarts God's purpose; rather, it polishes His instrument.*[4]

Delay proves our faith (Abraham) and purifies our character (Joseph). The next chapter discloses yet another benefit of delay and suggests what to do while we're waiting.

Dig Deeper

In this chapter, I quoted from V. Raymond Edman's *The Disciplines of Life*. In 1975, my New Testament professor, Merrill C. Tenney, told me he considered Edman the best devotional writer of his generation. Though the book was released over fifty years ago, you may be able to procure a copy online. The chapter on delay was one of several entries that ministered to me. On average, authors of previous generations offered more wisdom and less fluff than today's writers.

Read Psalm 37, which contrasts the security of those who trust in the Lord with the insecurity of the wicked. Which verses offer perspectives on, and suggested responses to, uncertain times?

CHAPTER 22

WINNING AT WAITING

The Discipline of Delay, Part 2

WHEN YOU SEE OR HEAR THE WORD "CURRICULUM," WHAT COMES TO MIND?

Church workers think of published materials utilized in Sunday school or small groups. They purchase lessons for various age-levels with coverage of biblical themes or books mapped out over a span of years in what's called a "Scope and Sequence." School staff associate the term with the sequence of courses a student takes.

In both venues, we connect *curriculum* to *content* covered. But the word literally means "racecourse." Figuratively speaking, it's the course students run in order to reach the finish line: obtaining a diploma or reaching a point of maturity.[1]

This broader definition suggests that a church's curriculum—the racecourse leader's map for members—includes worship services, missions projects, mentoring relationships . . . you name it! Any formal or informal opportunity that shuttles folks along spiritually is part of the church's curriculum. At the biblical university where I teach, the curriculum includes chapel assemblies, students' off-campus ministry, counseling services, faculty's non-classroom contact, sports, even life-style standards imposed by administrators.

This explanation clarifies for me a concept called *divine curriculum*: the figurative racecourse God maps out for his children, which consists of the people, experiences, and events he brings into our lives in order to develop us. His goals for us include Christlikeness (Rom. 8:29) and service (1 Pet. 4:10–11). The route he designs includes energy-sapping hills, unexpected turns, and only an occasional downhill slope that allows us to coast. The route is far from easy.

A challenging segment of the racecourse God plans for many of his servants is inexplicable delay. In the previous chapter, we saw how a frustrating time of waiting proved Abraham's faith and purified Joseph's character. Now the spotlight shifts to David and renowned missionary Hudson Taylor. Waiting wasn't a course they elected to take, nor did it show up on their tuition bill. Yet not even servants of their caliber could waive the requirement of delay. Let's discover what they learned.

Circuitous Route to the Throne

Probably a young teen in 1025 BC when Samuel anointed him King Saul's successor, David's road to the throne was long and arduous. To the highs of slaying Goliath and military conquests as a commander in Saul's army, add these lows:

- dodging spears thrown by a deranged Saul;
- living off the land and pleading for handouts during seven years on the run;
- saving himself ignominiously from Saul's army by feigning madness before the King of Gath, letting his saliva run down his beard;
- compromising for the sake of safety by residing among his old nemeses, the Philistines;
- and, hiding in caves

Does that sound like typical grooming for royalty? Did David wonder if Samuel had picked the wrong son of Jesse? What emotions roiled around inside David as he and his ragtag band of four hundred men kept their eyes peeled for Saul's soldiers?

Not until Saul died in 1000 BC did David take over in Judah, adding northern Israel to his reign a couple years later. A span of twenty-five years bridged his anointing by Samuel and his ascension to the throne. Why did God's plan for David move at a snail's pace? How did waiting profit David and expedite God's agenda?

Answering those questions requires inspection of the psalms David wrote while Saul was in hot pursuit. From his own pen I've culled the following benefits of delay in David's life.

1. *The threats David faced while waiting resulted in honest, heartfelt prayers.* Venting his anxiety and burdens served as a release valve for pressure. God as a refuge was experiential reality, not a doctrine known only through cognition.

While on the lam from Saul, crouched in a cave, he wrote, "My soul takes refuge in You" (Ps. 57:1). Perhaps from the same cave he said, "I cry aloud with my voice to the Lord. . . . I pour out my complaint before Him; I declare my trouble before Him. . . . I cried out to You, O Lord; I said, 'You are my refuge'" (Ps. 142:1–2, 5). David's advice to his readers wasn't glib, having practiced what he preached: "Cast your burden upon the Lord and He will sustain you" (Ps. 55:22).

2. *Trials David endured while waiting weaned him from circumstances as the basis for his security and joy.* He came to the God-pleasing point of finding soul-satisfaction through praise *before* his deliverance was assured. Writing—again from his respite in a cave—he exclaimed, "I will bless You as long as I live; I will lift up my hands in Your name. My soul is satisfied as with marrow and fatness, And my mouth offers praises with joyful lips (Ps. 63:4–5).

It's easy to praise God *after* he intervenes. It's passing a much harder test to honor him when predators lurk and you're shrouded in uncertainty. Habakkuk 3:17–18, written generations later, captures David's attitude:

> Though the fig tree should not blossom
> And there be no fruit on the vines,
> *Though* the yield of the olive should fail
> And the fields produce no food,
> Though the flock should be cut off from the fold
> And there be no cattle in the stalls,
>
> *Yet I will exult the Lord,*
> *I will rejoice in the God of my salvation* (emphasis mine).

3. *While waiting for his coronation, the furnace of adversity forged David's deep trust in the Lord.* He kept focusing on God's character, reminding himself of God's promises, and on multiple occasions saw him come to the rescue. The process instilled in David a rigorous faith he would need to survive a tumultuous forty-year reign.

The fears that faith in God assuaged in the wilderness prepared him for faith-threatening events in the latter half of life: "When I am afraid, I will put my trust in You. In God, whose word I praise; In God I have put my trust; I shall not be afraid. What can *mere* man do to me?" (Ps. 56:3–4).

In *Knowing God,* James I. Packer explains how painful situations, such as the delay David experienced, force us to rely on God. The Lord doesn't shield us from adversity because He wants

> to overwhelm us with a sense of our own inadequacy and to drive us to cling to him more closely. This is the ultimate reason, from our standpoint, why God fills our lives with troubles and perplexities of one sort and another: it is to ensure that we shall learn to hold him fast.[2]

4. God's divine curriculum of waiting produced an outcome that David didn't envision: *the Psalms he penned while enrolled in this course expanded his impact on future generations of believers.* I've found at least nine soul-nourishing, faith-sustaining psalms stemming from the years avoiding Saul's army: Psalm 18, 34, 52, 54, 56, 57, 59, 63, and 142. No military exploits or executive decisions wielded the influence these psalms have exerted for over three millennia.

―――――――――

Carol, nervous about delivering her first baby, sang Psalm 34:1–4 as a nurse wheeled her into the delivery room:

> I will bless the LORD at all times;
>> His praise will continually be in my mouth.
>
> My soul will make its boast in the LORD;
>> The humble will hear it and rejoice.
>
> O magnify the LORD with me,
>> And let us exalt His name together.
>
> I sought the LORD, and he answered me,
>> And delivered me from all my fears.

―――――――――

In the throes of a turbulent, three-year depression episode, Psalm 54:4 was a biblical anchor that kept me afloat: "Behold, God is my helper; the Lord is the sustainer of my soul." My despondency didn't evaporate when I memorized this verse and others, but their content instilled a God-centered, rather than a self-centered focus, enabling me to maintain a modicum of trust for a brighter future.

―――――――――

Though wracked by doubts and gut-wrenching pain, a couple I know who lost a child receives solace in Psalm 34:18: "The LORD is near to the brokenhearted and saves those who are crushed in spirit."

———————⇝———————

Multiply those stories exponentially and one conclusion crystallizes: the discipline of delay prepared David for, and released, fruitful service to the Lord.

Yet Bible characters don't monopolize this benefit.

Fruitful Setback

The delay in fulfilling his calling was unexpected and frustrating. After six years of intensive outreach in China, at age twenty-nine, Hudson Taylor returned to England—a furlough prompted by poor health. For five years he waited to return, all the while burdened by the spiritual darkness in China where thirty thousand died daily without hearing the Gospel.

In *Hudson Taylor's Spiritual Secrets*, his son, James, explains how those years of waiting tempered the steel of his father's soul. For periods of time in his London flat in a poor part of the city, Taylor and his family were "shut up to prayer and patience." Persevering prayer became a deeply ingrained habit. He experienced "the deep, prolonged exercise of a soul that is following hard after God. . . . [The] gradual strengthening, here, of a man called to walk by faith, not by sight; the unutterable confidence of a heart cleaving to God and God alone." As those years away from China progressed, when despondency assailed him, "prayer was the only way by which the burdened heart could obtain any relief."[3]

Yet the value of the delay wasn't restricted to the cultivation of deeper faith through desperate prayer. When his health permitted, he spoke in churches across the British Isles to promote the needs in China. Taylor helped translate the New Testament in a Chinese dialect. He received more medical training that he knew would come in handy in rural outposts of China. Most significantly, during persistent bouts of prayer, God's Spirit planted a vision to expand outreach in China by launching a new sending agency. In 1865, he founded China Inland Mission, which sixty-five years later became Overseas Missionary Fellowship. In 1866, after raising enough funds to support a team of twenty-one workers, Taylor sailed back to China, where he labored forty-five more years.

Initially, poor health and years away from his beloved Chinese appeared nonsensical—a detour from God's calling. But almost 150 years later, the missionary society he organized still penetrates unreached areas with the gospel. Rather than diminishing his effectiveness, delay multiplied it. Like David, delay prepared Taylor for greater long-term usefulness to God. This irony reminds me of a poem that comforts me concerning God's sovereign work when I'm hurting.

God Knows What He's About

When God wants to drill a man,
And thrill a man,
And skill a man
When God wants to mold a man
To play the noblest part;

When He yearns with all His heart
To create so great and bold a man
That all the world shall be amazed,
Watch His methods, watch His ways!

How He ruthlessly perfects
Whom He royally elects!
How He hammers him and hurts him
And with mighty blows converts him

Into trial shapes of clay which
Only God understands;
While his tortured heart is crying
And he lifts beseeching hands!

How He bends but never breaks
When his good He undertakes;
How He uses whom He chooses
And which every purpose fuses him;
By every act induces him
To try His splendor out.
God knows what He's about!

—AUTHOR UNKNOWN

David's psalms and the book by Hudson Taylor's son unveil our primary responsibility when God schools us in delay: *seek God through prayer*. Just as few folks trust God unless they *have to*, some of us don't pray fervently until life pulls the props out from under us and the Lord is all we have left.

May these perspectives on delay sustain you in *your* ministry, as they've buttressed my faith in my spheres of service.

Dig Deeper

As you read the two chapters on delay, to what extent did the content resonate with you? What personal experiences of waiting came to mind? How do the stories of Abraham, Joseph, David, and Taylor help you interpret what happened to you?

Now you see the past from the vantage point of the present. Precisely how did God use delay to prove your faith? To purify your character? To prepare you for expanded usefulness? If you've never thanked him for the fruit that stemmed from the soil of delay, pause and do so now.

Do you know a servant of God who is between vocational ministry positions? Whose labor appears fruitless? Who is impatient because God's pace is slower than he or she prefers? Ask the Lord for an opportunity to share the perspectives of these chapters on delay with him or her, along with your own testimony of God at work during a time of waiting.

Digest Psalm 62:5–8.

What words did David use to describe God?

How can these descriptors sustain you when you're waiting on him?

Which verse tells us what to do when we're agonizing over delay?

CHAPTER 23

Don't
Lose Heart

Why do Christian workers lose heart?

When I reflect on my own pilgrimage and on countless conversations I've had with church staff, missionaries, and volunteers, the following threats to endurance surface:

- feeling incompetent for necessary tasks,
- doubts about fruitfulness,
- stress of interpersonal conflicts,
- discouragement over one's own spiritual progress,
- weariness from overwork,
- rigorous opposition to goals or plans,
- physical infirmities that drain energy,
- despair over family members not following the faith,
- or emotional frailty that impedes productivity

Be ruthlessly honest. *What is the primary challenge to your own ministry resolve?*

The Apostle Paul's ministry was fraught with difficulty. Yet he pressed on. He finished well. What fueled his perseverance? He addressed that question in the fourth chapter of 2 Corinthians. He sandwiched helpful insights between two declarations of his steadfastness. In verses 1 and 16, Paul said, "We do not lose heart."

The Greek term for "lose heart" contains a root word that refers to evil or fallenness. Losing heart isn't limited to getting discouraged or burning out. The words may also allude to spiritual defection in the form of abandoning one's call, shirking one's duty, or disqualification due to blatant sin.

The following pages explain four reasons not to defect or yield to discouragement. These highlights represent selective insights I often preach to myself, not an exhaustive exposition of 2 Corinthians 4.

Ministry Is a Mercy

The New Testament term "mercy" connotes a compassionate response to need. In reference to God, it's an attribute that fosters positive treatment of us when we deserve the exact opposite. We know that mercy prompted God's plan of redemption and explains our salvation (Eph. 2:4; Tit. 3:5). Perhaps we're less cognizant of the role his mercy plays in our ministries.

In 2 Corinthians 4:1, Paul's recognition that his ministry was a mercy charged his battery: "Since we have this ministry, as we have received mercy, we do not lose heart." In 1 Timothy 1:12–16, Paul pointed out that God's mercy accounted for his call to service, as well as his conversion. Contrasting his zealous opposition to Christ with his apostolic commission, he emphasized, "I was shown mercy" (v. 13) and "I found mercy" (v. 16).

What are the implications of perceiving our ministry as a demonstration of God's mercy?

For me, the bottom line is that I'm totally undeserving of the outlets he has provided: two church staff positions, pulpit supply, overseas training of national workers, over three decades as a Christian university professor, bylines on articles and book jackets—*who am I to warrant such influential opportunities to serve a King!?*

I try to wrap my mind around this perspective when I catch myself sulking over others' treatment of me, when I throw a pity-party because I don't think I get enough respect or recognition, when I start complaining about a lack of responsiveness or compliance among persons I serve, or when I'm distraught over anemic results that fell way short of my expectations. I lose sight of the privilege that's mine, and the mercy God has exhibited in saving me and enabling me to serve him.

Pastor and author John MacArthur Jr. tells of a time when this "ministry is a mercy" outlook kept him from losing heart. At one point, 250 people left his church, calling his sermons too long and irrelevant.

> I was tempted to react in the flesh and say, "Those people don't appreciate me, I'm not going to take this!" and then go home to complain to my wife. The right response is, "I don't deserve to stand up and teach any of these people. If they *all* walked out next Sunday, I'd be getting what I deserve." It is a mercy I have not so affected my wife that she walked out. It is a mercy I have not somehow disappointed my children and made them turn away from Christ. It is a mercy I haven't stood in the pulpit and said such stupid things that my congregation ran me out of town![1]

Viewing my ministry as a mercy means I don't *have* to serve the Lord, *I get to do it!*

God Is My Audience

Nestled in 2 Corinthians 4 is a second heart-massaging insight. *We exercise all ministry "in the sight of God."* No matter who constitutes our primary target group—congregants, Bible study group participants, the unchurched—God is our principal audience when we serve.

In reference to his communication of God's truth, Paul commended himself "to every man's conscience in the sight of God" (v. 2). In 2 Corinthians 2:17, Paul declared, "For we are not like many, peddling the word of God, but as from sincerity, but as from God, we speak in Christ in the sight of God." He reiterated this perspective one other time in this letter: "It is in the sight of God that we have been speaking in Christ; and all for your upbuilding, beloved" (2 Cor. 12:19). Imagine: if you're a Bible teacher, everyone except God is just eavesdropping!

If false motivations spur what we do, or if we settle for mediocrity instead of striving for excellence in our spheres of service, knowing God is watching may legitimately convict us. Since accountability before God is entwined in this concept, we're less likely to lose heart in the sense of moral defection or rebellion against a call to a difficult task. But knowing we minister in the sight of God also blocks discouragement. That's because, even when we're disappointed in outcomes, he sees that we gave it our best effort. He remembers our faithfulness to the task and rewards us accordingly. Though others may fail to recognize or appreciate our efforts, that's not the case with God. Hebrews 6:10 reveals his keen memory and offers a hint of divine compensation: "God is not unjust so as to forget your work and the love which you have shown toward His name, in having ministered and in still ministering to the saints."

Viewing the Lord as my primary audience also provides a buffer against mistreatment from the very folks I'm striving to serve. I'm less prone to quit, knowing I'm first and foremost serving *him* and showing love *to him* through what I do. In his classic devotional *My Utmost for His Highest*, Oswald Chambers echoes this point: "The mainspring of . . . service is not love for men, but love for Jesus Christ. If we are devoted to the cause of humanity, we shall soon be crushed and broken-hearted, for we shall often meet with more ingratitude from men than we would from a dog; but if our motive is love to God, no ingratitude can hinder us from serving our fellow men."[2]

Frailty Doesn't Disqualify Us

Physical and emotional weakness comprise the main challenge to my own perseverance. Years of sleep deprivation siphon off energy for teaching and church work, necessitating a couch in my office where I can stretch out and close my eyes for a few minutes most afternoons. Despite thousands of dollars spent on medical treatments, spinal degeneration spawns pain that often feels like my spine is in the vise-grip of giant pliers. For days at a time, depression envelops me, depleting passion and making every chore more difficult. But reading 2 Corinthians 4 reminds me I'm not alone, and instills hope.

Paul described the human body in which God's Spirit and the message of the gospel reside as "earthen vessels" (2 Cor. 4:7), a term describing plain, valueless, fragile containers that concealed precious commodities, such as gold currency.[3] He went on to say that he was "always carrying about in the body the dying of Jesus" (v. 11) and that "death works in us" (v. 12). He added that "our outer man is decaying" (v. 16).

Why does this acclamation of human frailty encourage me? Paul cites a providential reason for our weakness: "We have this treasure in earthen vessels, *so that the surpassing greatness of the power will be of God and not from ourselves*" (v. 7, emphasis mine). Verse 11 conveys the same slant. We're feeble and physically descending toward death "that the life of Jesus may also may be manifested in our body." He uses us despite weaknesses so *he*, rather than we, looks good in the process. People realize that the only explanation for our accomplishment is that *God did it.* Commentator Philip Hughes elaborates on this reassuring emphasis:

> It is one of the main purposes of this epistle to show that this immense discrepancy between the treasure and the vessel serves simply to attest that human weakness presents no barrier to the purposes of God. . . . Weakness is a challenge to power. The extent of God's power is such that it overcomes

and transcends all man's weakness: the former is not merely sufficient to counterbalance the latter, but it goes beyond and far exceeds it.[4]

That's why Paul stopped trying to yank out his "thorn in the flesh" and instead started boasting about his physical limitation. Jesus told him, "My grace is sufficient for you, for power is perfected in weakness" (2 Cor. 12:9). Paul concluded, "When I am weak, then I am strong" (v. 10).

An incident in Jack Murray's life showed that weakness is not a hindrance to usefulness. His son, George, told this story in chapel while he served as President of Columbia International University.

Jack, a traveling evangelist, was coming off back-to-back weeks of meetings in local churches. He boarded a plane, headed to yet another week-long engagement. The intensive delivery of messages and constant interactions with people had depleted his mental and physical reserves. Craving a nap so he could recoup, he was delighted to hear that seating was open rather than assigned. Since the plane was only half full, to signal his desire for privacy, he sat by a window, placing his coat and hat on the two adjacent seats.

Surprisingly, a sharply-dressed business woman asked to sit in the aisle seat next to him. She tried to engage Jack in conversation, but he cited the exhausting week behind him and said he needed to rest during the flight. He pushed the seat-recliner button, closed his eyes, and leaned his head against the bulkhead. That's when someone else started talking to him.

"Jack, there's a woman sitting next to you," whispered God's Spirit.

"Yea, I know. And of all the places she could have selected, she sat next to me!"

"Don't you think that's significant?" asked the Lord.

"But Lord, You know how tired I am!" Jack countered. He contended with the Lord for several minutes, then yielded to his wooing. After asking forgiveness for his attitude, he pushed the seat button, sat upright, and opened his eyes. Immediately the lady blurted, "Oh, are you feeling better?"

A casual conversation ensued. When she said she lived and worked in Charlotte, North Carolina, Jack mentioned a friend of his: Henderson Belk, president of the Belk department store chain, headquartered in her city. Excitedly, she announced that she worked for Mr. Belk in the corporate office. "Have you noticed anything different about your boss lately?" Jack inquired.

"Oh, yes. Everybody is talking about him. He 'got religion' or something," she said. That's when Jack explained how Mr. Belk had recently put his faith in Christ. He shared the gospel with her and her heart began to melt. She wept, revealing a broken heart over dysfunction in her family. She didn't pray to receive Christ on the plane, but Jack made her promise to ask her boss about what happened to him. Within a week, Henderson Belk cultivated the soil where Jack had planted a seed, and led his employee to faith in Christ.

When Jack was at the end of himself due to physical frailty, he and the woman were at the beginning of God's grace. Instead of stemming the flow of God's power, his weariness merely created a dependency on it.

Focus on the Future

From 2 Corinthians 4, I glean one more concept that nourishes resilience. I rely on it when skirmishes with Satan leave me battered and I cower before his relentless attempts to mar my witness and public ministry. I need it when the gravitational pull of my sinful heart slams me to the mat, eroding my resistance. When frustration with others' apathy swells, enhancing the appeal of resigning. When doubts about my impact stifle motivation.

During such moments, I inject this powerful antidote into my failing heart: *limitations, frustration, battles—they're all temporary!* God's Spirit whispers, "Hang on a while longer. This won't last forever."

Paul anchored his hope in a future beyond the realm of time and space in which he served, declaring, "He Who raised the Lord Jesus will raise us also with Jesus" (v. 14). He viewed current stressors through the lens of eternity: "Momentary, light affliction is producing for us an eternal weight of glory far beyond all comparison, while we look not at the things which are seen, but at the things which are not seen; for the things which are seen are temporal, but the things which are not seen are eternal" (vv. 17–18).

The distance runner who concentrates on the finish line perseveres through lung-gasping, muscle-cramping pain. The boxer entering the final round wards off debilitating fatigue because he knows the bell that ends the match is only three minutes away. Similarly, the beleaguered Christ-follower who's being pummeled by temptation doesn't cave in because he knows this life is brief and the next one isn't. He realizes that any day he could be on the verge of seeing Jesus face-to-face. The Christian worker stays faithful because he lives expectantly. He's aware of a deadline. Either physical death will usher him into Christ's presence or he will return, sparking a raucous celebration.

Our bodies won't ache forever. Temptation and discouragement won't always dog us. The tears generated by the devastating effects of sin will one day dry up (Rev. 21:4). I've read my Bible all the way to the end, and we who know and serve Christ win. To the eternal perspective in 2 Corinthians 4, add Hebrews 10:36–37:

> For you have need of endurance, so that when you have done the will of God, you may receive what was promised.
>
> FOR YET IN A VERY LITTLE WHILE,
> HE WHO IS COMING WILL COME, AND WILL NOT DELAY.

Our hope of eternal life is what Gabriel Marcel defines as "a memory of the future."[5] This kind of hope means we are just as convinced about what will happen (the future) as we are of what has already occurred (the past).

That's why we don't lose heart.

Dig Deeper

One of the books from which I extracted a quote for this chapter is *Stand: A Call for Endurance of the Saints* (Crossway, 2008). This book teems with insights to keep God's people from losing heart. Contributors who tell the secrets to their endurance within *Stand* include John Piper, Justin Taylor, Jerry Bridges, John MacArthur, Randy Alcorn, and Helen Roseveare. Devour the tips from leaders who've persevered. You'll highlight or underline something on every other page. Read it with a pen in your hand.

CHAPTER 24

SOURCE OF YOUR SIGNIFICANCE

OVER A FIVE-YEAR PERIOD, JAKE'S YOUTH GROUP TRIPLED. HIS EFFERVESCENT PERSONALITY DREW KIDS AND HE knew how to speak their language. He devoted several nights a week to events he planned and to hanging out with them. Jake often spoke at conferences so others could benefit from all that God was doing in his ministry. When it came to youth work, Jake always gave 100 percent.

That's why his wife took the kids and left him. She said there isn't much left after 100 percent.

$$\rightleftharpoons$$

When Rhonda teaches the Bible, ladies listen, expectantly. Extraordinary knowledge complements her incisive communication skills. Except Rhonda doesn't know how to receive a compliment. When a participant expresses appreciation for the study, a typical reply is, "Thank you, *but* . . ." Rhonda goes on to apologize for a three-second lapse in concentration, for one ambiguous question she posed, or for a cross-reference she couldn't retrieve from her memory bank. If the PowerPoint equipment failed or if she groped for the answer to an unanticipated question from a group member, she resorts to self-recrimination.

———————※———————

Ron confided why he left the pastorate to work in a parachurch organization. It boiled down to his inability to please enough people. He said he felt good about himself only when church members liked or complimented him. Ron felt like soft taffy, pulled in different directions by influential congregants who had their own agenda for the church. He used others to verify his worth as a person.

———————※———————

When he received a negative student evaluation for a course he taught, Randy sank into a slough of despondency that lasted for days. A long history of positive evaluations as a Christian college professor didn't prevent an emotional form of vertigo that left him reeling. Their unfavorable opinion of his course sapped him of joy and weakened confidence needed for other teaching venues.

———————※———————

A workaholic youth director.

A gifted, but self-absorbed, perfectionistic Bible teacher.

A church leader plagued by an excessive yearning to please.

A university professor with a fragile ego, whose self-image hinges on students' perception of him.

Undoubtedly, complex psychological factors spawned those attitudes and behaviors. Yet it's clear-cut that all four persons exhibit an insecure personal identity. They rely on success or others' opinions for feelings of worthiness. Despite their love for God and commitment to ministry, their sense of significance isn't based on a biblical premise.

Due to our sin and the fallen world in which we live, we'll never have it all together spiritually or psychologically this side of heaven. Yet grasping the implications of a foundational biblical truth can infuse us with a healthier self-concept, nudging us closer to emotional maturity. When we dissect this doctrine, our true identity crystallizes. The irony is that Jake, Rhonda, Ron, and Randy all know this truth. Without looking it up, they can define it. They've taught it. But there's a gulf between their comprehension and application of it. Data stored in their cognitive realm hasn't seeped into their affective domain. (To some extent, each of us teaches beyond our level of experience.)

Perhaps a fresh look at this facet of salvation will help shuttle it from our heads to our hearts. On the axis of *redemption*, everything in relation to our identity shifts.

Purchase Price

To redeem means "to buy back," to reclaim ownership of an item by paying for it. If you're desperate for quick cash, you take your family heirloom or TV to a pawn shop. The clerk gives you a portion of its value in cash, along with a pawn ticket, keeping the item as collateral for the loan. If you return by the deadline, you use your ticket to redeem your valuable. The shop gets their money back, plus a hefty interest payment. For an inflated price, you obtain what was originally yours.

In the New Testament era, the term *redeem* referred to the purchase of a slave. The connotation is that our plight prior to salvation was one of slavery. Originally we were God's creation, his possession. But sin entered the picture, enslaving us to Satan. *Redemption* means God "bought us back."

First Peter 1:18–19 discloses the purchase price: "You were not redeemed with perishable things like silver or gold from your futile way of life . . . but with precious blood, as of a lamb unblemished and spotless, *the blood* of Christ." Paul echoed the same point about the transaction for our souls: "In Him we have redemption through His blood, the forgiveness of our trespasses, according to the riches of His grace" (Eph. 1:7).

My favorite text on the concept of redemption doesn't actually contain the word. In an argument for sexual purity, Paul said, "Do you not know that your body is a temple of the Holy Spirit who is in you, whom you have from God, and that you are not your own? *For you have been bought with a price*: therefore glorify God in your body" (1 Cor. 6:19–20, emphasis mine).

When I fail the Lord, causing self-loathing to surface, or when I catch myself relying on accomplishments or others' feedback to determine my worth, I meditate on a principle from Marketing 101: *a product is worth what someone is willing to pay for it.*

In 2013, the Seattle Mariners pro baseball team gave pitcher Felix Hernandez a historic contract: $175 million, spread over seven years. They figured he's worth the money, having won the league's Cy Young award as best pitcher in 2010, and having pitched a perfect game in 2012.

The Baltimore Ravens, 2013 National Football League Champions, awarded quarterback Joe Flacco a six-year, $120.6 million contract. They based his worth to the team on precision passing that catapulted them to a Super Bowl victory. A television commercial during that same game in 2013 cost advertisers an average of $3.5 million for a thirty-second spot. The worth of an ad depends on the size of the viewing audience.

By the time you read this, the escalating salaries of top professional athletes probably cause what Hernandez and Flacco received to pale by comparison.

Jesus' death on the cross unveils the intrinsic worth of a human soul. The corrective to low self-esteem, to feelings of unworthiness, is theological. *How precious is Christ the Son to God the Father? His life is the price paid for our salvation.* Now we're God's property, and whatever (or whoever) he owns, he cherishes. Whoever heard of royalty paying an exorbitant price for something (or someone) insignificant?[1]

Owning Redemption

The verb "to appropriate" means "to set apart for a specific use" or "to take possession of." A Christian worker who appropriates redemption goes a step beyond comprehension, putting intentional effort into applying it.

We "own" redemption when we meditate on its meaning and invite the Holy Spirit to shuttle it from our head to our heart. We ask him to reveal indicators that we're basing our identity and sense of well-being on performance or others' opinions of us. We serve *because* God loves and values us, not in an attempt to prove our worth. To a greater extent than before, we're able to enjoy the gospel, not just peddle it. Though we strive for excellence, mistakes or inadequacies provide an opportunity to revel in God's grace. We stop short of falling into a downward cycle of self-condemnation.

Secure in our identity as the Lord's property, and ever conscious of the high price Christ paid for fellowship with us, we frame the following credo and put it where we'll see it every day: *"Nothing to Prove. Nothing to Lose."*

But I can't sign off on this chapter before citing one more Bible passage revealing the source of our significance.

His Work or Mine?

While in high school, Sam boldly shared his faith with unchurched friends. People kept coming to Christ as a result of his aggressive but winsome witness. One teen who converted to Christ through Sam's testimony became a pastor, then a missionary to Haiti for twenty-two years.

But when Sam attended a public university, results were harder to come by. He presented the gospel just as often, yet few expressed interest in Christ. Discouragement enveloped Sam. Perplexed by their apathy, he thought God had abandoned him. Sam kept checking his spiritual pulse to determine what was wrong. The exuberance that had characterized his walk with Christ eluded him.

Then the Lord spoke to Sam during a devotional time in Luke 10. Jesus sent seventy followers to share the Gospel in a number of cities and villages. Jesus instructed them on how to behave when people were receptive, and how to respond if folks rebuffed their message (vv. 8–11). When the seventy returned, they couldn't keep a lid on their excitement. Their glowing report of success included victory over the forces of Satan: "Lord, even the demons are subject to us in Your name" (v. 17).

Jesus' reaction to their report brims with meaning to everyone whose sense of worth depends on ministry performance: "Do not rejoice in this, that the spirits are subject to you, but rejoice that your names are recorded in heaven" (v. 20).

Mulling over Jesus' words pricked Sam's conscience. He confessed that the source of his joy and basis for his self-worth were misplaced. He had been relying not on the work of Christ for his identity, but on the results of his personal evangelism.

When we read Jesus' remark on verse 20 from the perspective of his subsequent death on the cross, we're informed by this inescapable conclusion: *the source of our significance is not what we do for Christ, but what he has already done for us.*

Now *that's* a sermon worth preaching to yourself!

Dig Deeper

When a nonfiction Christian book sells in the millions, we know it taps into a sense of felt need. If this "Source of Your Significance" chapter resonates with you, get a copy of Robert S. McGee's *The Search for Significance: Seeing Your True Worth Through God's Eyes* (Nelson, 2003). McGee addresses false beliefs about human significance and bases our identity in the work of Christ. He explains how the doctrines of justification, redemption, reconciliation, propitiation, and forgiveness should affect our view of God and self. A separate workbook and devotional journal accompany this bestseller.

An older volume to peruse is Maurice E. Wagner's *The Sensation of Being Somebody: Building an Adequate Self-Concept* (Zondervan), first released in 1975. He discloses the causes and symptoms of an unhealthy self-concept, and like McGee, roots a sound identity in biblical truth. Wagner showed me how basing my sense of significance on anything else but the gospel hinders selfless service and restricts my capacity to love others unconditionally. When my identity isn't secure, I use others to affirm my own worth. My need for their compliments hinders authentic love for them.

Dr. Bill Jones, president of Columbia International University, wrote *Discovering Your Identity*. This workbook delves into doctrines to help the reader resist false cultural values that shape most folks' personal identity. Each chapter focuses on a different biblical truth and offers a blend of Bible study questions and commentary. There's a separate twelve-session *Leader's Guide* for small-group facilitators or adult Sunday school teachers.[2]

BALANCING INPUT WITH OUTPUT

THE DEAD SEA IS A LAKE OCCUPYING THE SOUTHERN END OF THE JORDAN RIVER VALLEY. ITS NORTHERN TIP RESTS near the city of Jerusalem. This sheet of greenish salty water is eleven miles across at its widest point and almost fifty miles long. The water itself is marked by a distinctively bitter taste and a nauseous smell.

Do you know why it's called the "Dead Sea"? The water contains so many minerals, such as bromide and sulphur, that few living things can survive in it. This happens for one basic reason: *the Dead Sea has inlets, but no outlets.*

Millions of tons of water—from the Jordan and several smaller streams—flow into the basin daily. This salty sea would be fresh or only mildly saline had it an outlet, but that hot and arid climate serves as a gigantic evaporating pan. Flooding is prevented because the dry heat rapidly evaporates the water.

This fact about the Dead Sea reflects a truth of Christian living: *we need to construct outlets so that whatever blessings and biblical truths flow into our lives eventually refresh others as well.* Our lives aren't as vibrant, reproductive, and attractive if what we're learning isn't channeled toward others with whom we have contact.

If God's Spirit has utilized the content of *Serve Strong* to nourish your soul, the next few pages offer a few ideas for outlets. Select at least one of the following means of refreshing others with what you've learned.

Personal Reflections

Before brainstorming with you on ways to encourage others with the book's content, pause and reflect on its impact on you. Employ the questions that follow as catalysts for your thinking. The questions overlap, yet each probe may jog your memory in a different way.

- What biblical principle in *Serve Strong* reassured or encouraged you most? Why?
- What feelings and attitudes surfaced as you read? Why?
- What chapter in your book has the most highlighted or underlined sentences? Why did that chapter's content resonate with you?
- Which truths or Bible passages spawned prayers of gratitude or praise to God? What personal circumstances did these truths or verses address?
- Which illustration from the book is easiest to remember? Why did that story leave an indelible impression?
- How did material in *Serve Strong* magnify God's grace and sufficiency for persons involved in ministry?
- Did anything you read influence any ministry-related decisions? (Did you back off plans to quit? Did something prompt you to accept a new service opportunity?)

Your motivation to communicate the Bible truths in *Serve Strong* to others depends on your experience of God's sustenance through these insights.

Now let's shift to venues and means of encouraging others with the content. Which one you select depends on the position or opportunities for influence God has given you.

First-Class Communication

Send a hand-written letter to a church volunteer, a church staff member, or a missionary you know. Express gratitude for this person's ministry and say that you want to pass along a biblical insight that touched you personally. Explain the truth in your own words, and how God's Spirit applied it to you. Close the letter by writing out a prayer for the recipient.

Staff Devotions

When you meet with your church or parachurch staff, utilize Scripture and principles from *Serve Strong* during your group devotional time. Choose the insights most pertinent to the felt needs and responsibilities of those under your supervision.

Interactive Bible Study

Here's a skeletal plan for a thirty to forty-five minute group Bible study. Employ it in a staff meeting, at a retreat, or during a training event for Bible study leaders.

"Encouragement for Those Who Serve"

Introduction:

Tap into a sense of felt need by discussing this question: *What factors cause discouragement to persons involved in ministry?*

Bible Study:

Each set of Bible verses that follow offers at least one biblical perspective to help us combat discouragement. If a set shows more than one reference, both passages convey or reinforce the same truth. Distribute the verses among members of your group and ask all of them to find an answer to this question: *What reason for encouragement or boost to ministry motivation does this scripture offer?*

Beside each set of verses, I've listed the chapter where I covered that passage. You can crystallize, deepen, or supplement their replies as needed. (This is far from an exhaustive list of passages cited in the book, so feel free to revise it as you wish.)

- Isaiah 41:10; Hebrews 13:5 (Chapter One, "He Promised His Presence")
- Psalm 50:15 (Chapter Ten, "How God Gets Glory")
- Hebrews 6:10 (Chapter Twenty-Three, "Don't Lose Heart")
- 2 Corinthians 3:5–6 (Chapter Three, "But God")
- Jeremiah 23:29; Hebrews 4:12 (Chapter Two, "The Power Is On")
- Galatians 6:6–10 (Chapter Seventeen, "Reaping What You Sow")
- 1 Corinthians 15:58 (Chapter Twenty, "Promise Keeper")
- 1 Corinthians 1:26–29 (Chapter Nine, "Captain of the *Are Nots*")
- 2 Corinthians 12:9–10 (Chapter Eleven, "Harnessing Our Potential")
- Acts 16:11–15; 1 Corinthians 3:1–7 (Chapter Eighteen, "The Pressure Is Off")

Response Time:

Invite volunteers to tell which Bible passage or truth means most to them right now and why. Close the study with prayers of gratitude to God for the nourishment his Word provides.

Formal Presentation

Are you scheduled to speak at a retreat for Christian workers? At a conference for women's ministry leaders? At a church's "Volunteer

Appreciation" dinner? Are you a pastor who wants to bolster the spirit of congregants who serve as Sunday school teachers, board members, musicians, and small group leaders?

Then take a few of the Bible texts and truths explained in *Serve Strong* and deliver a message titled, "Encouragement for Those Who Serve."

You're capable of selecting your own Bible passages and illustrations, but, as an example, here's the outline of a message I gave at a local church. In case you want to adapt it, I list the correlated chapter in *Serve Strong* for each point. Reviewing those chapters will enable you to add the muscle of commentary and stories to the skeleton I'm providing.

Introduction:

Cite factors that cause discouragement or waning motivation among folks who serve God. Emphasize that you'll share perspectives that buoy your own spirit as a worker.

I. **God Pledges His Presence** (Chapter One)
   A. Scripture: Isaiah 41:10; John 14:16; Hebrews 13:5
   B. Story: Joseph

II. **God Provides Us with Adequacy** (Chapter Three)
   Scripture: 2 Corinthians 3:5–6; Philippians 2:13

III. **God Picks Unlikely People** (Chapter Nine)
   A. Scripture: 1 Corinthians 1:26–29
   B. Story: Dwight L. Moody

IV. **God Pierces with His Word** (Chapter Two)
   A. Scripture: Jeremiah 23:29; Hebrews 4:12
   B. Story: Charles Spurgeon "testing the acoustics"

V. **God Promises Eternal Dividends** (Chapters Seventeen and Twenty)
   Scripture: 1 Corinthians 15:58; Galatians 6:6–10

Conclusion:

See story of "chain reaction" of ministry impact from Kimball (1850s) to the work of Billy Graham (Chapter Seventeen).

Gift Book

Ask the Lord to give you the name of a Christian vocational worker or volunteer who could use a dose of encouragement. Give this person a copy of *Serve Strong*. Write a personal note in the front expressing gratitude for the recipient's faithful ministry.

Decades ago I heard Stuart Briscoe say, "God doesn't bless you or teach you solely for your own benefit." If God's Spirit encouraged you through the insights in *Serve Strong,* I hope you'll take Briscoe's words to heart and funnel this material to others in your sphere of influence.

Endnotes

Introduction:
Preaching to Yourself

[1] "Sermons from God," Clean Jokes, ChristiansUnite.com, accessed March, 2011, http://jokes.christiansunite.com/Sermons/Sermons_from_God.shtml.

[2] "Sermon Humor," Javacasa.com, accessed October 6, 2013, http://javacasa.com/humor/sermon.htm.

[3] In *Future Grace* (Multnomah, 1995), John Piper introduced me to the concept of "preaching to yourself." See Chapter Twenty four, titled "Faith in Future Grace vs. Despondency." He expanded on David Martyn Lloyd-Jones' emphasis on "biblical self-talk" in *Spiritual Depression: Its Causes and Cures* (Grand Rapids: Eerdmans, 1965).

Yet another helpful resource promoting emotional and spiritual health through right thinking is William Backus and Marie Chapian's *Telling Yourself the Truth: Finding Your Way out of Depression, Anxiety, Fear, Anger, and Other Common Problems by Applying the Principles of Misbelief Thearpy* (Minneapolis: Bethany House, 1980). Brisk sales of their book for over three decades show how much their material resonates with people.

Part One: When You Wonder if It's Worth It

Chapter 1:
He Promised His Presence

[1] Mark Buchanan, *The Holy Wild: Trusting in the Character of God* (Colorado Springs: Multnomah, 2005), 62. I heartily recommend all of Buchanan's books, especially *The Rest of God: Restoring Your Soul by Restoring Sabbath* (Nelson, 2007) on the Sabbath principle for God's people today. He's the rare local church pastor who's also a word carpenter when he writes. His books teem with fresh verbs and metaphors, as well as engaging content.

Chapter 2:
The Power Is On!

[1] D. Stuart Briscoe, *Titus: Living as God's Very Own People* (Wheaton: Harold Shaw, 1994), 83.

[2] Samuel Johnson, quoted in Briscoe's *Titus*, 84.

[3] Literally, Pastor Flavel said, "Many of you are *'Anathema Maranatha'* because you love not the Lord Jesus Christ." I merely captured the essence of his words.

[4] Charles H. Spurgeon, *Lectures to My Students, The Art of Illustration*, vol. 3 (Lynchburg: The Old-Time Gospel Hour), 47–48.

[5] Eric W. Hayden, "Charles H. Spurgeon: Did You Know? A Collection of True and Unusual Facts about Charles Haddon Spurgeon," *Christian History* 29 (1991): 1–3. A pastor who succeeded Spurgeon at the Metropolitan Tabernacle reported this story.

Chapter 3:
But God . . .

[1] V. Raymond Edman, *But God* (Grand Rapids: Zondervan, 1962), 13–14.

[2] John Piper, *Future Grace* (Sisters, Oregon: Multnomah, 1995), 302.

Chapter 4:
Netless Followers

[1] Joseph M. Stowell, *Shepherding the Church of the 21ˢᵗ Century: Effective Spiritual Leadership in a Changing Culture* (Wheaton: Victor Books, 1994), 112.

[2] John Piper, *Desiring God: Meditations of a Christian Hedonist* (Sisters, Oregon: Multnomah, 2011), 240.

[3] Ibid.

[4] John Piper, as quoted in a blog titled "Jesus Makes Up for Every Sacrifice" by David Mathis at the *Desiring God* website, http://www.desiringgod.org/blog/posts/jesus-makes-up-for-every-sacrifice. Accessed October 27, 2012.

Chapter 6:
Playing Back God's Call

[1] John Piper, *The Roots of Endurance: Invincible Perseverance in the Lives of John Newton, Charles Simeon, and William Wilberforce* (Wheaton: Crossway Books, 2002), 129.

[2] Ibid., 130.

[3] Ibid., 128.

[4] Ibid., 137.

Chapter 7:
Rousing the Enemy

[1] If you research the topic of "spiritual warfare," you'll encounter widely divergent views on how warfare manifests itself and how to achieve victory over Satan. Perhaps the most biblical and balanced resource I've consulted is David Powlison's *Power Encounters: Reclaiming Spiritual Warfare* (Grand Rapids: Baker Books, 1995). He desensationalizes the popular subject of "demonic deliverance" without slipping into an unbiblical rationalism that has little room for the devil's power.

More recently, former missionary and president of the Southern Baptist International Mission Board, Jerry Rankin, wrote *Spiritual Warfare: The Battle for God's Glory* (Nashville: B&H, 2009). Strengths of his book include anecdotes of Satan's activity on the mission field, the emphasis on Satan's use of deceit that makes believers more susceptible to temptation, and his assertion that the root of all spiritual conflict is Satan's desire to diminish the glory of God.

As the narrative describing Jesus' temptation suggests (Matt. 4:1–11), *fasting* is a vital weapon to strengthen us for spiritual battles. The best book on the subject that I've read is John Piper's *A Hunger for God: Desiring God through Fasting and Prayer* (Wheaton: Crossway, 1997).

C. S. Lewis' *The Screwtape Letters* is a classic on Satan's deceptive tactics against God's people. Put it on your top-ten "bucket list" of books to read this side of heaven.

[2] Gary Thomas, *Thirsting for God: Spiritual Refreshment for the Sacred Journey* (Eugene: Harvest House, 2001), 203.

[3] Jerry Rankin, *Spiritual Warfare: The Battle for God's Glory* (Nashville: B&H, 2009), 8.

Chapter 8:
The Blessing Factor

[1] Bob Counsins, *Experiencing LeaderShift: Letting Go of Leadership Heresies* (Colorado Springs: David C. Cook, 2008), 172.

[2] Ibid., 243.

[3] Ibid., 174.

Part Two: When You Feel Inadequate

Chapter 9:
Captain of the *Are Nots*

[1] Paul Dwight Moody, *The Shorter Life of D. L. Moody* (Ann Arbor: University of Michigan Library, 1900), quoted in "Dwight L. Moody," wikipedia.com, accessed June, 2013, http://en.wikipedia.org/wiki/Dwight_L._Moody.

[2] Ibid.

[3] Richard Day, *Bush Aglow: The Life Story of Dwight Lyman Moody, Commoner of Northfield* (Valley Forge: Judson Press, 1936), 9.

[4] Ibid.

[5] Ibid.

[6] F. W. Grosheide, *The First Epistle to the Corinthians*, The New International Commentary on the New Testament, ed. F. F. Bruce (Grand Rapids: Eerdmans, 1953), 52.

[7] John Piper, "Brothers, Read Christian Biography," *Desiring God* Web site, accessed January 1, 1995, http://www.desiringgod.org/resource-library/articles/brothers-read-christian-biography.

Chapter 10:
How God Gets Glory

[1] John Piper, *God's Passion for His Glory: Living the Vision of Jonathan Edwards* (Wheaton: Crossway, 1998), 32.

[2] *Desiring God*, 144, 140.

[3] *God's Passion for His Glory*, 43.

[4] Charles Spurgeon, quoted in *Future Grace*, 301.

[5] Ibid.

[6] Charles Spurgeon, quoted in Randy Alcorn's blogs, Eternal Perspectives Ministries. "Depression, Gratitude, and Charles Hadden Spurgeon," September 4, 2007; "More on Depression in the Christian Life and Ministry," September 11, 2007. Accessed March, 2013.

[7] Arnold Dallimore, *Spurgeon* (Carlisle, Pensylvania: The Banner of Truth Trust, 1984), 220.

[8] Charles Spurgeon, quoted in Piper, *Desiring God*, 140.

[9] Charles Spurgeon, quoted in Piper, *Future Grace*, 9.

Chapter 11:
Harnessing Our Potential, The Blessing of Brokenness, Part 1

[1] Alan Nelson, *Embracing Brokenness: How God Refines Us through Life's Disappointments* (Colorado Springs: NavPress, 2002), 18.

[2] Vance Havner, *Pepper 'n' Salt: Homey Stories, Humor, Inspiration, and Bible Otulines, Savored by One of America's Most Beloved Evangelists* (Grand Rapids: Baker, 1966), 20.

[3] Ray C. Stedman, *Authentic Christianity* (Grand Rapids: Discovery House, 1996), 124.

[4] Gary Thomas, *Thirsting for God* (Eugene: Harvest House, 2011), 131–132.

[5] Ibid., 132.

Chapter 12:
Wanted: Wounded Soldiers, The Blessing of Brokenness, Part 2

[1] I firmly believe that medical intervention and counseling are forms of God's "common grace" to mankind. My 2003 experience of surrender doesn't mean I never avail myself of those two resources for chronic depression. Though as of this writing I have been off anti-depressants for years, I still visit a Christian counselor occasionally to help me deal with negative thought patterns and receive objective input on issues I'm facing. My submission to God's sovereignty over my despondency was essential for me but it doesn't preclude my striving for emotional stability. What it means is that I'm willing to accept God's will even when my efforts don't work.

[2] Adapted from Henry and Richard Blackaby and Claude King in *Experiencing God: Knowing and Doing the Will of God* (Nashville: B&H, 2008).

[3] Dennis Cochrane, in a chapel address at Columbia International University in 2005.

[4] You can access audio and visual presentations by the late Buck Hatch at the archives of Columbia International University, www.BuckHatchLibrary.com.

[5] Nathan Hatch, "The Gift of Brokenness." *Christianity Today* (November 14, 1994), accessed May, 2012, http://www.christianitytoday.com/ct/1994/november14/4td034.html. All other quotations in this section of the chapter are also from Nathan's article.

[6] From personal notes of a message delivered by Joe Aldrich at a pastors' conference I attended at Wheaton College, summer 1975.

Chapter 13:
Failure Is Not Final

[1] H. G. Anderson, "John Mark," in *Zondervan Pictorial Encyclopedia of the Bible*, ed. Merrill C. Tenney, vol. 4 (Grand Rapids: Zondervan, 1975), 89.

[2] John Wesley, "The Nature of Idolatry," sermon, The Bible Truth Chat Room, January 27, 2012, accessed May, 2013, http://bibletruthchatroom.com/2012/01/the-nature-of-idolatry/.

[3] From my personal notes of a sermon titled "The Ministry of Failure," as delivered by Ronald Dunn at a retreat for Campus Crusade for Christ staff in the 1970s. I heard a tape of this message.

[4] From an August 7, 2013 blog by Bryan Lowe, "John Newton—Great Quotes To Ponder." Cross Quotes, CrossQuotes.org. Accessed October 24, 2013.

[5] James I. Packer, *Knowing God* (Downers Grove: InterVarsity Press, 1973), 219–220.

Chapter 14:
The Power of Owning Up

[1] When I refer to weaknesses or flaws in the lead to this chapter, I'm not referring to a blatant moral lapse that would dishonor God's name. Some sins *do* disqualify us from public ministry. Some weaknesses or failures reflect a heart condition that requires healing and restoration or a leave of absence from our sphere of service until we're whole again.

[2] In 1972, Larry Richards framed an entire book to volunteer teachers around Naomi's teaching adventures: *You, The Teacher* (Chicago: Moody Press). He used her story to promote a relational approach to teaching and a personal touch in the classroom. You may still find copies of *You, The Teacher* from Amazon.com or Alibris.

[3] Larry Richards, *A Theology of Christian Education* (Grand Rapids: Zondervan, 1975), 142.

Chapter 15:
The Ministry of Pain

[1] Lloyd Shearer, "Children Who Feel No Pain," Intelligence Report, *Parade Magazine*, February 12, 1989, 18–19.

[2] From a taped message titled "Becoming Usable," delivered by Ronald Dunn to the staff of Campus Crusade for Christ, late 1970s.

[3] Jonathan Edwards, *The Life of David Brainerd*, ed. Norman Pettit, *The Works of Jonathan Edwards*, vol. 7 (New Haven: Yale University Press, 1985), 186.

[4] Ibid., 541.

[5] John Piper, *The Hidden Smile of God: The Fruit of Affliction in the Lives of John Bunyan, William Cowper, and David Brainerd* (Wheaton: Crossway, 2001), 155.

[6] Ibid., 132.

[7] Nelson, *Embracing Brokenness*, 166.

Chapter 16:
The Tracks of Your Tears

[1] Leonard Ravenhill, *Why Revival Tarries* (Minneapolis: Bethany House, 1991).

[2] Joe Bayly, "Why Don't Sinners Cry Anymore?" *Eternity* (Oct. 1974): 71–72. Bayly wrote a regular column for this periodical.

[3] J. Kenton Parker, "How McCheyne Preached," in Paul Lee Tan's *Encyclopedia of 7700 Illustrations* (Rockville: Assurance Publishers, 1979), 1430.

[4] R. A. Torrey, "Give Me Back My Tears," ibid., 1429.

Part Three: When You Don't See Results

Chapter 17:
Reaping What You Sow

[1] R. C. Sproul, *Essential Truths of the Christian Faith* (Carol Stream: Tyndale House, 1992), xxiv. His thirteen-page introduction to the book makes an excellent case for the teaching of doctrine and sketches ten causes that work against the Christian goal of spiritual maturity.

[2] Not all published reports of the "chain of conversions" leading from Edward Kimball to the salvation of Billy Graham are factually accurate. Yet the ripple effect that connects Kimball's witness to Moody to the 1934 conversion of Graham is undeniable.

What I wrote stems from these sources:

- The Billy Graham Center archives of Wheaton College: "Who led Billy Graham to Christ and was it part of a chain of conversions going back to Dwight L. Moody?" March 31, 2005. Accessed June 2012.
- Chapman, J. Wilbur (1859–1918), Presbyterian Historical Society. Accessed June, 2012.
- Hy Pickering, "Conversion of Wilbur Chapman: A World-Wide Evangelist," Wholesome Words: Christian Biography Resources, accessed April, 2011, http://www.wholesomewords.org/biography/bchapman2.html.

Chapter 18:
The Pressure Is Off

[1] Charles Swindoll, *Growing Strong in the Seasons of Life* (Portland: Multnomah, 1983), 80.

[2] Oswald Chambers, *My Utmost for His Highest* (Newark, Delaware: Dodd, Mead and Company, 1936), 114.

[3] From an e-mail I received from David Cashin on January 21, 2010.

Chapter 19:
Liberation from the Success Syndrome

[1] Charles Swindoll, *Growing Strong in the Seasons of Life* (Portland: Multnomah, 1983), 147.

[2] Charles Colson, quoted in Kent and Barbara Hughes, *Liberating Ministry from the Success Syndrome* (Wheaton: Crossway, 2008), 37–38.

[3] Rankin, *Spiritual Warfare*, 103–04.

[4] From a personal conversation with Robertson McQuilkin on the theme of this chapter.

Chapter 20:
Promise Keeper

[1] Dallas Willard, *The Spirit of the Disciplines: Understanding How God Changes Lives* (New York: Harper and Row, 1988), 150, 177.

Chapter 21:
Delays Are Not Denials, The Discipline of Delay, Part 1

[1] Ron Dunn, "The Ministry of Failure: Deuteronomy 8," Lifestyle Ministries, 2005, ronndunn.com/the-ministry-of-failure/.

[2] Merrill C. Tenney, *Roads a Christian Must Travel: Fresh Insights into the Principles of Christian Experience* (Carol Stream: Tyndale, 1979), 27.

[3] Charles Spurgeon, *Psalms: Volume II.* The Crossway Commentary Series, ed. Alister McGrath and J. I. Packer (Wheaton: Crossway, 1993), 92.

[4] V. Raymond Edman, *The Disciplines of Life* (Wheaton: Victor Books, 1948), 80–83.

Chapter 22:
Winning at Waiting, The Discipline of Delay, Part 2

[1] Lois LeBar, *Education That Is Christian* (Wheaton: Victor Books, 1989), 254. This edition of Dr. LeBar's classic included fresh insights for families, churches, and schools by Dr. James E. Plueddemann.

[2] Packer, *Knowing God*, 222.

[3] Dr. and Mrs. James Taylor, *Hudson Taylor's Spiritual Secrets* (London: China Inland Mission, 1932), 75.

Chapter 23:
Don't Lose Heart

[1] John MacArthur, "Certainties That Drive Enduring Ministry," *Stand: A Call for the Endurance of the Saints*, ed. John Piper and Justin Taylor (Wheaton: Crossway, 2008), 57.

[2] Chambers, *My Utmost*, 54.

[3] Philip E. Hughes, *Paul's Second Epistle to the Corinthians*, The New International Commentary of the New Testament (Grand Rapids: Eerdmans, 1962), 136.

[4] Ibid.

[5] Gabriel Marcel, quoted in Carol J. Kent, *When I Lay My Isaac Down: Unshakable Faith in Unthinkable Circumstances* (Colorado Springs: NavPress, 2004), 108.

Chapter 24:
Source of Your Significance

[1] Any time I write or speak on the subject of a Christian's self-concept, I qualify my remarks with this overarching biblical perspective: *God doesn't exist for our sake; we exist for his sake.* The capstone of all biblical theology is *his* glory and worth, not ours. "Not to us, O Lord, not to us, but to Your name give glory because of Thy loving-kindness, because of Your truth" (Ps. 115:1).

When our personal identity or significance isn't set in the solid concrete of Jesus' work on the cross, the result is emotional instability and selfish motives for ministry. But I'm not advocating a self-centered, consumer mentality in the church. God's priority is to showcase himself, not us. Balance the human worth couched in the doctrine of redemption with these words from John Piper: "The love of God for sinners is not his making much of them, but his graciously freeing and empowering them to enjoy making much of him." *God's Passion for His Glory*, 34–35.

[2] Order a copy through Crossover Communications International, 7520 Monticello Road, Columbia, SC 29203 (803-691-0688).

About the Author

Since 1981, Terry has taught in the Church Ministries program at Columbia International University in South Carolina. He's been on the staff of three churches for a total of twelve years. Terry has written or co-authored eighteen books and scores of articles. He has trained workers in thirteen countries and over twenty-five states in the areas of Church leadership and Bible teaching.

Availability

Terry Powell can serve your church, denomination, or organization through pulpit supply, retreats, or leadership development seminars. In addition to the themes in *Serve Strong,* he specializes in training leaders in the areas of church ministry issues and leading group Bible studies. Consult his Web site for a full listing of conference themes and topics: www.terrydpowell.com. Contact him personally at Columbia International University: 803-807-5453 or tpowell@ciu.edu.

Blog and Resources

Terry also writes a weekly blog at www.terrydpowell.com. This site features free resources, including articles he's written on Christian living, church ministry, or Bible teaching; devotionals; faith poems; Bible study guides for groups, and more. A number of his blogs, articles, and poems wrestle with maintaining virile faith in times of despondency.